CAUSALITY IN ECONOMICS

CAUSALITY
IN ECONOMICS

John Hicks

Basic Books, Inc., Publishers

NEW YORK

Library of Congress Number: 79–7346
ISBN: 0–465–00900–X
Copyright © 1979 by Sir John Hicks
Printed in the United States of America
10 9 8 7 6 5 4 3 2 1

CONTENTS

Preface

When I was introducing my book about *Economic History*[1] I could claim that, although I am no historian, I had read a good deal of history; in introducing this one I can make no corresponding claim. When I was an undergraduate student, I read the philosophical classics, such as they were given to us in Oxford in the twenties, but I have not kept up with my reading in that field. So the subject of this book is not one which I have kept in my cupboard, mulling over it for years (as Harrod said he had done with his *Foundations of Inductive Logic*); I came upon it quite recently, and rather suddenly. How that was I will try to explain.

I took part, in 1974, in a conference on the 'Micro-Foundations of Macro-economics', an International Economic Association conference at S'Agaro in Spain. The proceedings of that conference have subsequently been published. Though some excellent papers were given, reviewers have rightly perceived that the conference as a whole was a failure. We did not get to grips with the question we were supposed to be discussing. I could see that at the time, and as I came away I was asking myself why.

One of the reasons, I became convinced as I thought

---

[1] A Theory of Economic History (1969).

it out, was that the question had been wrongly posed. It took for granted that 'micro' (the economics of the firm and of the individual) was a solid foundation, on which the more dubious 'macro' (economics of the whole economy, usually a national economy) was to be built. What were the grounds for holding that the one was more solid than the other? We were begging that question, but we should have faced it. To have discussed the foundations of economic theory in general was perhaps too large, and too divisive, a matter for discussion among a group. Heart-searching of that kind is better conducted by oneself. An intermediate inquiry might nevertheless have been possible; we might have discussed, without attention to 'micro', the foundations of macro-economics.

What is macro-economics for? This is a more special question than what economic theory is for; some of the answers which, to judge from their practice, economists would give to the latter question are clearly ruled out.

There is much of economic theory which is pursued for no better reason than its intellectual attraction; it is a good game. We have no reason to be ashamed of that, since the same would hold for many branches of pure mathematics. But macro-economics is not a particularly good game. It is true that there are some problems, of purely intellectual interest, which seem to come out of it; but if one pursues them very far, one feels that one is on the wrong track.[2] They are not characteristic of macro-economics.

---

[2] I have twice had experience of this myself. Both in the course of working at my *Trade Cycle* book (1950) and in the course of working at *Capital and Time* (1974) I found myself involved with convergence problems which were mathematically interesting. I could not refrain from giving them some attention, though I felt that they were questions which, in view of the nature of my models, I ought not to be asking.

Secondly, there is a part of economic theory which is pursued for the sake of ideology; it is concerned with ideal arrangements, whether of the Left or of the Right. There is something of that in the work of Keynes, who is the father of modern macro-economics; but in the work of his successors (those who would regard themselves as macro-economists) it has faded out. Macro-economics is more down to earth than that.

In the third place, there is optimum theory, allocation theory, 'given ends and scarce resources'. In some of its forms, as sometimes in welfare economics, it gets close to ideology. It has nevertheless been shown that it can be realistic, as in its offshoot cost-benefit analysis; and it has something to say which can be of use for business management. But it does not have much to do with macro-economics. Links between them may exist, but they are tenuous.

What then is left? There are two main uses which seem to be left. One is descriptive. The concepts of macro-economics are used, all the time, for summarizing experience, not only by statisticians, but also by politicians and by journalists. One of the tasks of the economic theorist is the criticism of such concepts: the refinement of a pure measure of national income (for instance) and the study of the relation between the pure measure and the practical, or popular, measures which stand proxy for it. I do not question the importance of this activity, but it is not the use with which I shall be here concerned.

The other use is the analytical use, which perhaps after all is central. I do not mean analysis in the sense in which all theory is analysis; I am thinking of analysis applied to facts. When theory is applied, it is being used as a means of explanation: we ask not merely what happened, but why it happened. That is causation; exhibiting the story, so far as we can, as a logical

process. How does one do that? How can one do that?
It was by that route that I was led to causality.

Having got that far, I had to stand back from
economics. The study of causation is much wider than
economics; it is what science is about, and what much
of history is about. So I could not say what I wanted to
say about economics, and indeed about macro-
economics, until I had taken a stand on much wider
questions. That is why in this book I have started, as it
were, from outside.

All that is said about economics, in the first three
chapters, is from outside. I use economics as an illustration, but hardly more than an illustration. So I am
hopeful that some of the things which are said in these
chapters (and also in Chapter VIII, on probability)
will be of interest to others than economists. I have
ventured to give some examples, from outside
economics, but I am very conscious that they are
amateurish.

Then, in Chapters IV–VII, I turn to look at economics more particularly, in the light of what I have
been saying. Some quite interesting points, which I
had not myself suspected before I started on this
inquiry, seem to emerge. If one is firm in judging
theories not by their intrinsic beauty, nor by their
value in supporting (or confuting) ideologies, but by
their usefulness as means of explanation, one must
classify them according to the kinds of problems (of
real problems) to which they claim to have relevance.
Many of the disputes among theorists can then be
referred to the interests of those who construct them,
in different problems. This approach turns out to be
particularly helpful in relation to disputes between
'static', 'quasi-static' and 'dynamic' theories. I find
that all experimental sciences are, in the economic
sense, 'static'. They have to be static, since they have
to assume that it does not matter *at what date* an

experiment is performed. There do exist some economic problems which can be discussed in these terms; but there are not many of them. The prestige of scientific method has led economists to attach importance to them, for this is the field where economics appears to be most 'scientific'. The more characteristic economic problems are problems of change, of growth and retrogression, and of fluctuation. The extent to which these can be reduced into scientific terms is rather limited; for at every stage in an economic process new things are happening, things which have not happened before—at the most they are rather like what has happened before. We need a theory that will help us with these problems; but it is impossible to believe that it can ever be a complete theory. It is bound, by its nature, to be fragmentary. It is commonly called 'dynamic' in contrast to 'static'; but that is a name which now seems to me to be better avoided. For 'dynamics', in its original sense, is a branch of mechanics; and the problems, to which the economic counterpart (if it is a counterpart) refers, are not mechanical. As economics pushes on beyond 'statics', it becomes less like science, and more like history.

I believe that this line of thought helps one to transcend the Byzantine disputes among the various schools of 'neo' economists. One can draw, at least approximate, boundaries between their fields of relevance. As has been found in the political field, it is safer to have boundaries, even if they are not always respected.

There is however another aspect of the scientific invasion, to which I come in Chapter VIII. The probability calculus, which is a powerful tool of discovery in the sciences, has seemed in recent years to be carrying all before it in economics also. No piece of research, in economics, seems now to be regarded as respectable unless it is decorated with least squares and confidence intervals. It is my belief that the relevance of these methods to economics should not be taken for granted; before they are applied, their use should be defended. There is evidence that this was the view of Keynes himself.[3] He would not have been surprised to find that after the boom in its activities which we have experienced, econometrics is now in some disarray. I try, in Chapter VIII, to show why.

The acknowledgements which I have to make are rather sketchy. Most of the work that has gone into this book has been done in my own study, without much discussion with others. An early version of these ideas was, however, presented at a seminar at Princeton, during a brief visit to the United States in January 1978; what was then said about it by Fritz Machlup gave me much encouragement to go on. Discussions with Gary Hawke, of the University of Wellington, New Zealand, who was then a Visiting Fellow of All Souls, were very useful to me, at much the same time. There are passages in a near-final version which have been usefully criticized by Carlo Casarosa, of Pisa, Italy, whose stay in Oxford began at the time when I was finishing; and I have had similar help from my colleague at All Souls, Geer Stuvel.

[3] See his famous review of Tinbergen in 1939 (reprinted in his *Collected Writings* Vol. XIV, pp. 306–20). Though some of his points have been answered in later work by econometrists, there is a core that remains. It should be remembered, in reading that review, that Keynes was the author of *A Treatise on Probability* (1921).

CAUSALITY IN ECONOMICS

I
Why Economics?

Causality and economics, which I have joined in my title, are words that are not often found together. Causality, the relation between cause and effect, is thought to be the business of philosophers; economists, though they often talk about effects and sometimes (perhaps less frequently) about causes, are usually content to leave the question of the meanings of these terms to others. I have come to think that this is a pity. For I have come to think that its apppearance in economics is a particularly interesting, and particularly revealing, case of the general notion of causality. It should be useful to economists, for whom I am mainly writing, to have clearer ideas about it; but the clarification, though mainly directed at the economic application, should be of use to others also.

I can see three reasons why the economic application is particularly instructive. It will be the purpose of the present chapter to set them out.

The first is the simple fact that economic knowledge, though not negligible, is so extremely imperfect. There are very few economic facts which we know with precision; most of the 'macro' magnitudes which figure so largely in economic discussions (Gross National Product, Fixed Capital Investment, Balance of Payments and so on—even Employment) are subject to errors, and (what is worse) to ambiguities, which are far in excess of those which in most natural sciences would be regarded as tolerable. There are few economic 'laws' which can be regarded as at all firmly based. Now for the purpose of the present inquiry these things are advantages. The degree of certainty which we attribute to some of the generalizations (and predictions) of the natural sciences is such that it is hard to distinguish it from logical necessity; we are as certain that the sun will rise tomorrow[1] as we are that two and two make four. No one can attach that degree of certainty to any economic prediction. Even the lesser degree which attached to predictions in meteorology or medicine is in economics far to seek. Economics is a leading example of uncertain knowledge; it is knowledge, yet it is evidently uncertain. Now if we are able, at least in some relevant aspects, to understand the significance of uncertain knowledge, we can proceed from that to incorporate the case of near-certain knowledge, merely by diminishing the degree of uncertainty. If, however, we take the case of near-certain knowledge as our typical case (especially if we allow ourselves to neglect the—perhaps very small—degree of uncertainty which accompanies it) we are bound to find it much harder to proceed to uncertain knowledge, which then appears as radically different. So that is the first reason why it is profitable to take the case of economics, its position on the edge of the sciences.

The second is the relation between economics and time. A property which was stated by David Hume[2] to

---

[1] Interpreting this as meaning that the earth will continue to rotate. If the statement is taken as a definition of tomorrow, it is a logical necessity, indeed a tautology.

[2] *Treatise of Human Nature*, Part 3, Section 2. (*Philosophical Works*, ed. Green and Grose, Vol. I, p. 378.)

be 'essential to causes and effects' is that of 'priority in time in the cause before the effect'. I do not myself believe (as in the next chapter I shall be explaining) that this property is as 'essential' as Hume thought it to be; but that the relation of cause and effect has some reference to time is undeniable. Now the mere fact that the economist is so largely concerned with current affairs, the affairs of the present, gives him a particular responsibility with respect to time. It is a responsibility which is akin to that of the historian. What the past is to the historian, the present is to the economist. The work of each of them is in time, in historical time, as the work of most natural scientists is not.

Experimental science, in its nature, is out of historical time; it has to be irrelevant, for the significance of an experiment, at what *date* it is made, or repeated. There are indeed some sciences, non-experimental sciences, which have their own calendars. Astronomers are beginning to fix the dates at which their stupendous events have probably happened; geologists to fix dates at which changes have occurred in the crust of the earth. But on their timescales human life is no more than a speck; when they say something happened so many years ago, it does not matter whether one is measuring from the invention of writing or from the year 1979. The whole of recorded history, for them, is in the present. But the economist's present is our present—the day through which one is living, or the hour that is striking as one writes.

That present is fleeting; one does not have time to think about it before it is past. So if one says that the economist is concerned with the present, that is just another way of saying that he is concerned with the past *and* with the future. Recent past and near future; but near future is still future and recent past is already past. Last year's statistics are historical statistics.

There is accordingly an overlap between the work of the economist and the work of the historian. For there is no logical difference between the study of recent history and the study of the history of earlier periods. The same principles must apply to each.

The economist is concerned with the future as well as with the past; but it is from the past that he has to begin. It is the past that provides him with his facts, the facts which he uses to make his generalizations; he then uses these generalizations as bases for predictions and for advice on 'planning'. In purely historical work, the latter element is missing, or is at least less prominent; though it is easy to name historians who desire to draw from the past some lessons for the present and future, lessons which may be implied rather than stated, yet do not differ in principle from those which the economist draws. I think not merely of the 'philosophers of history', such as Spengler or Toynbee, but also of the element of concern with the problems of their own time which is traceable in more regular historians, such as Gibbon or Rostovtseff, not to mention our contemporaries! But even though this element may be present in the work of historians, it is always less central than it is in the work of economists. The historian is concerned with the past, in its relation to the present; the economist is concerned with the present, and for the sake of the present with the past.

Economics, accordingly, if it is on the edge of the sciences (as we saw) is also on the edge of history; facing both ways, it is in a key position. So a consideration of economics, in the way we shall be considering it, may throw light in both directions.

It may indeed be objected that the same key position is occupied by other social sciences, political science and sociology; like economics, they are on the edge of science and on the edge of history. There is however a third reason for the claim I am making for economics, a reason which other social sciences do not share in the same way. Economics is specially concerned with the making of decisions, and with the consequences that follow from the decisions; the implications of this are profound.

Take the field which (as just shown) is common to economics and history: the study of the past, with the object of finding out, not only what happened, but why it happened. That is causality; if the study is successful, it should enable us to state a cause; we should be able to say that A caused B. Now A, in history (in political history, as in economics) will often be a decision, that someone made; B will be the consequences which we state to have followed from the decision (so that here there is no question but that cause and effect are sequential). The search for a cause of this type will be a question of identifying the particular decision from which B, some recorded events, are supposed to have followed. Or perhaps (but more often in the historical than in the economic case) it will be sufficient to identify who it was that made the decision—who it was that was responsible.

There is clearly an analogy with the proceedings of a court of law. Someone was murdered; who was the murderer? The extent to which such legal, or moral, conceptions have influenced the writing of history, and not only the writing of history, is notable. It may indeed be said that up to the eighteenth century looking at causes and effects in a theologico-legal manner was almost universal. Every event (or at least every important event) must either be the act of some person, who was thus responsible for it, or it must be an 'Act of God'. The latter, in modern usage, is not taken literally; no one, whatever his religious beliefs, would now maintain that the lawyer's 'acts of God' are particularly distinguished by divine origin. The survival of the term is nevertheless a reminder that there was a time when it meant what it said. It originated in a time when men understood very little of the things that surrounded them; so whenever the human agent was not obvious, his place was taken by an agent who was 'supernatural'. There was indeed a tendency to expand the range of things that were ascribed to human agency; it was not always a fortunate tendency, since the mediaeval habit of ascribing any death that could not be explained to the administration of poison—by someone!—is a leading example. One can yet distinguish a system of thought (we might call it the *Old Causality*) in which causes are always thought of as actions by someone; there is always an agent, either a human agent or a supernatural agent.

It is fascinating to observe, in the literature of the seventeenth and eighteenth centuries, how this Old Causality broke down. The human actions, it was supposed, were either Good or Evil; but what of the moral quality of the supernatural actions? To the more faithful representatives of the Old Causality that was a question which must not be asked; but it was inevitable that some should ask it. To 'justify the ways of God to men' was a task that had to be attempted; the heroic failure that is expressed in *Paradise Lost* is a part of the story. So is the Leibnitzian optimism of Pope's *Essay on Man*; God acts through natural laws, and the laws are good, though their consequences may be deplorable. But why should the laws be good? They enable us (usually) to earn our daily bread, but they are also responsible—if the word is appropriate—for such purposeless disasters as the great Earthquake at Lisbon, on which Voltaire wrote his poem, a crushing reply to Pope. The end of the Old Causality was then in sight.

The solution was found by the philosophers of the Enlightenment, Hume and Kant, to whom the historians, such as Gibbon,[3] should I think be added. It *was* the solution; for whatever the attitude which may now be taken towards the rest of their work, their New Causality was a permanent acquisition. It was the 'Old' association between Causality and Responsibility which had to be rejected. Causality is a matter of explanation; but when we explain, we do not necessarily praise or condemn. Having explained, we may proceed to praise or condemn, if we find it appropriate to do so; but the range of matters to which the category of cause and effect is appropriate is wider than that of those to which praise or blame can possibly be appropriate. Explanation and approval (or disapproval) are separate issues.

What then do we mean, in terms of the New Causality, if we assert that A caused B? A, we may take it, is some event that occurred at some time in the past, and B is some event which here we will still allow to have occurred at some later time. We will take it that we

---

[3] On the strength, in particular, of his famous chapters (15 and 16) on the rise of Christianity. Gibbon, we know, was an admirer of Hume; the letter which Hume sent him on the publication of the first volume of the *Decline and Fall* (which included these chapters) 'overpaid' he says in his *Autobiography* 'the labour of ten years'. Gibbon's analysis, in terms of 'natural' causes, met, as this letter shows, with Hume's approval. To the orthodox, of that time, it was shocking; not so now. It is instructive to set beside it the account of Christian origins, treading, one would think, on even more dangerous ground than Gibbon's, which is to be found in Vol. XI of the *Cambridge Ancient History*. 'Being absolutely convinced of the supernatural mission of Christ and his apostles' says Canon Streeter of the author of *Acts* 'the canon of probability which he naturally applies in the acceptance of stories involving miracles is the opposite of that of a modern historian.' Canon Streeter was a priest of the Anglican church. Hume and Gibbon have won through.

have satisfactory evidence that both of these events did actually occur.[4] For causality, we must be maintaining that if A had not existed, B would not have existed; if not-A, then not-B. But not-A and not-B are not events which have happened; they are events which have not happened. (In recent discussions among historians they are described as 'counterfactual'.) So they must be regarded as theoretical constructions; we cannot say anything about them unless we have some theory of the way things are connected. (It may be a very rudimentary theory, but it is a theory all the same.) In a statement of causality, theory is being *applied*.

I shall have much to say later about the application of theory; here I will merely note one important thing which the New Causality brings out. It could be asserted, if one held to the Old Causality, that every event must have a cause; it must be caused by some action, either human or supernatural. Could it be asserted, in terms of the New Causality, that every event must have a cause? Causation can only be asserted, in terms of the New Causality, if we have some theory, or generalization, into which observed events can be fitted; to suppose that we have theories into which *all* events can be fitted, is to make a large claim indeed. It was nevertheless a claim that thinkers of the eighteenth century, dazzled by the prestige of Newtonian mechanics, were tempted to make; not, even then, that knowledge of 'natural laws' was already complete, but that it was on the way to completion; a complete system of natural law seemed just round the corner. The laws in which 'God' expressed himself, according to Pope, must form such a system, a complete system. Hume, however, being himself a

---

[4] That, of course, was one of the issues; the rejection of supernatural causes was in part a question of evidence.

philosopher-historian, not a philosopher-scientist (like Descartes and Leibniz) was untempted by such imaginings; he knew full well how incomplete our knowledge of the 'laws' that causality requires must be. But just because it is incomplete, it is capable of being improved. And there are no bounds to the improvement that one may attempt to undertake; there are no events which one may not attempt to explain.

Which brings me back to economics. When Adam Smith called his book *An Inquiry into the Nature and Causes of the Wealth of Nations*, he must have been thinking in terms of the New Causality. For Adam Smith, like Gibbon,[5] was a friend of Hume's; modern economics, like modern historiography and (one can now see) modern philosophy, takes its origin from that same circle. Economics, ever since that day, has been committed to the New Causality, to the search for 'laws', or generalizations, on the basis of which we can assert something about the causes of events. It is a search which in the case of economics is most obviously never-ending; for economics, as I began by saying, is a characteristically imperfect science. The relation of economics to the New Causality is nevertheless rather special. For economics is concerned with actions, with human actions and decisions, so that there is a way in which it comes nearer to the Old Causality than the natural sciences now do. The struggle between free will and determinism, which was such a burning issue in the latter days of the Old Causality,[6] is still of relevance to economics. But in economics we find a solution.

It is a matter of what may be called the relativity of time.

We learn, in very elementary mechanics, of the

---

[5] And Turgot.

[6] It is in fact the central theme of *Paradise Lost*.

relativity[7] of motion. If, as in planetary astronomy is so convenient, we treat the sun as fixed, the earth is in orbit round the sun, and itself rotating. With respect to the sun, all human beings and all the objects that surround them are in rapid motion. We have to learn that this is by no means inconsistent with my personal observation that the furniture in the room where I am writing is at rest, while it is the sun that is moving. The simplicity of the Copernican model has caused it to displace in the minds of most modern men the understanding of planets and stars, by their appearances, which was familiar before Copernicus, and which is needed, even by modern man, if he is to observe the heavens, and not to allow others to do his astronomy for him. But it is not easy, even in this familiar case, to maintain the double vision.

In much the same way, though not exactly the same way, the historian himself is working at a particular time, with all that happened before that time already in the past and what is to come after it still in the future; he has nevertheless to transport himself in his mind to other dates, which have different pasts behind them and futures before them to those which he has now. If he is a pure historian, he can go to his date in the past—his 'period'—and stay there; so he need not be much perplexed by a need for double vision. But for the economist, who is aware that he is studying the past for the sake of the present, the double vision is a necessity. He is always under the necessity of looking at the past in the two ways, from its point of view and from his own; or, as he has learned to say, *ex ante* and *ex post*.

It is through this double vision, once he can attain it, that he is enabled to transcend the old controversy

---

[7] A much more elementary sense of relativity, of course, than Einstein's.

between Voluntarism and Determinism. People (you or I or our masters) do make decisions now, with an eye to the future. There is no reason, when looking forward, to doubt that we are free, as we feel ourselves to be, to choose one course of action rather than another. But no decision made now can affect what *has happened* in the past. Decisions were made in the past, but *now* they are past events. They cannot be affected by what is decided now, so there can be no free will about them—now. So, with respect to the past, one can be fully determinist. That is to say, as we have seen, there are no events in the past that one may not attempt to explain. Voluntarism, applied to the past, takes one back to the Old Causality; it can only be interpreted as meaning that there are some events in the past (past decisions) which the investigator is forbidden to examine. Determinism, applied to the future (in theological terms, pre-destination) is equally cramping; but determinism, applied to the past, is not cramping. It is liberating.

II
The Kinds of Causality

I now proceed to a closer examination of the definition of causality by 'not-A implies not-B'. So far, this is
no more than an outline of a definition; it needs much
further refinement before we can use it.

A is some event, occurring at some time (T_a); B is
some event occurring at some time (T_b) which we will
still for the present accept to be a later time. It is first
of all implied in the statement that 'A caused B' that A
and B did actually exist (or happen). This sounds
obvious; but it is not hard to find examples of alleged
causation where the mere existence of the 'cause' or of
the 'effect' turns out to be doubtful. For the one,
consider the alleged 'supernatural' causes that were
previously mentioned; and for the other, the economist is not unfamiliar with wild goose chases after causal
explanations of 'phenomena' which turn out to be
nothing more than mistakes which were made in the
statistical office. So the mere existence implication
must not be overlooked.

It must next be noticed that T_a and T_b do not have to
be moments of time; they can be periods of time, even
quite long periods. Thus it is quite proper to say that
the unusual lack of balance between the sexes in the
population of Britain in the nineteen-thirties was
caused by the First World War.

It is evident from this example that one cause may have many effects; and it is similarly evident (take the war to be the effect and look for its causes) that one effect may have many causes. The statement that A caused B is thus to some extent ambiguous. It may mean that A was one of the causes of B ('weak' causation) or it may mean that A was the sole cause of B ('strong' causation). Strong causation implies weak causation; but it also implies that there is no other potential cause which is admitted to be *a* cause of B. So it is a combination of weak causation for A with a denial of weak causation for other candidates.

So it is the definition of weak causation that is basic; once that is firmly established, we can build up strong causation from it (so far as we need to do so). But even in the case of weak causation we must make a further distinction.

There are two kinds of weak causation: *separable*, in which A is stated to be *a* cause of B, by itself, and *non-separable*, in which A is not stated to be more than a part of a separable cause. I shall have much to say about *non-separable* causation later; *separable* causation is simpler, so with it I shall begin.

If A is to be a separable cause of B, we must be able to conceive of a hypothetical situation in which A did not happen, but all other events (all other potential separable causes) were the same as did occur at time T_a. It is implied in the assertion of separable causation that such a situation can be (theoretically) constructed; only when that is granted can one proceed to the final step, of asserting that if that situation had been actual, at time T_a, then at time T_b B would not have occurred.

So there are *four* distinguishable elements in the assertion of (separable) causation of B by A. (1) A existed (2) B existed (3) the hypothetical situation in which A did not exist, *ceteris paribus*, can be constructed (4) if that situation had existed, at time T_a, B would not have occurred. All four are necessary; for though the fourth is critical, it makes no sense unless we grant the third. And unless the first two are granted, all that we get from the third and fourth is a theoretical statement, which establishes no causal connection, by itself.

I shall call the construction, defined under (3), the 'not-A construction'; for it has proved to be the meaning that has to be attributed, when we are thinking more precisely, to the 'not-A' from which we began. If not-A can be constructed, and with not-A B would not have happened, I shall say that A *passes the test*; granted that A and B exist, A is shown to be a separable cause of B.

Now let us go on to consider the case of two possible (separable) causes, which I will call A_1 and A_2. When we construct not-A_1, A_2 is among the *other things* which have to be equal; so A_1 passes the test if B would not have occurred when A_1 was absent while A_2 was present. A_2 passes the test if B would not have occurred when A_2 was absent while A_1 was present. These are different tests; so there is no inconsistency if causation by A_1 and causation by A_2 are asserted together.

Does it follow, however, that if both are asserted, B would not have occurred if A_1 and A_2 had both been absent? (I shall denote this construction by 'not-A_{12}'.) In most cases, one would suppose, it would follow; separable causes are usually additive. But they do not need to be additive; it is not hard to find cases where additivity breaks down.

They are, it turns out, of more than one type. For consider the following table, in which I write '+' for occurrence of B and '−' for non-occurrence. There are three tests, by not-A_1, by not-A_2 and by not-A_{12}; so in principle there are *eight* possibilities. (I include in my table an 'actual' column, for the 'actual', in which A_1 and A_2 both occur, and B occurs; so all entries in this coloumn are +.)

	Actual	Not-A_1	Not-A_2	Not-A_{12}
1	+	−	−	−
2	+	−	+	−
3	+	+	−	−
4	+	+	+	+
5	+	+	+	−
6	+	−	+	+
7	+	+	−	+
8	+	−	−	+

The first possibility (1) is straightforward; A_1 and A_2 pass the test, both separately and together. The effect will not appear unless both causes are present; they are *additive* causes. In case (2) A_1 passes but A_2 does not; it is indeed irrelevant whether A_2 is present or not; so A_1 (out of A_1 and A_2) is *sole* cause. Similarly, in case (3) A_2 is sole cause. In case (4), inserted for completeness, neither is a cause. None of these cases gives any trouble; if causation was always additive, any of these cases could arise.

The other cases are more peculiar, but they cannot be excluded. (5) is the case of *overlapping* causes. In case (1) the effect does not occur unless both A_1 and A_2 are present; in case (5) it occurs if *either* is present. There is no reason why this should be ruled out. The victim died after taking two poisons, either of which would have been sufficient to kill him. It could happen. The writers of detective stories are quite fond of it happening.

One does nevertheless have a feeling that it is an exceptional case, and there is a reason for that. We have been assuming that A_1 and A_2 have the same time reference—that they are contemporaneous.

Suppose however that they do not have the same time-reference; A_1 preceded A_2. In case (1) this makes little difference. It is true that after A_1 the effect does not immediately occur; it does occur after A_2, so A_2 (as we say) is the immediate cause. But it would not have taken effect if there had not been A_1 previously. The effects are additive, whether the causes are spread out in time, or are contemporaneous.

But in case (5) with A_1 preceding A_2, the effect occurs as a result of A_1; A_2 is irrelevant. Thus case (5) can be assimilated to case (2). It is only when the causes are contemporaneous that case (5) has to be distinguished.

This, we shall find, is a point of some importance; but before pursuing it further, let us look at the other cases, (6) to (8).

In each of these cases, it will be observed, there is a + in the 'not-A_{12}' column; B (we say) would have occurred, even if A_1 and A_2 were both absent. In this they are like case (4) where it had to be asserted that neither was a cause; so we would have to look for some other cause than A_1 or A_2. Here also we would have to look for some other cause; let us call it A_3, so 'not-A_{123}' would be marked with a –. Cases (6) to (8) must thus be read as cases where there are three causes; it is the interaction of the three which gives them their peculiar character.

Three causes might be simply additive, as in case (1); or they might be overlapping, either together or in pairs, as in case (5). What is asserted in case (6) is that though B would have happened if neither A_1 nor A_2 was present (but A_3 was present) and did happen when A_1, A_2, and A_3, were all present, it would not have happened in 'not-A_1', that is to say, when A_2 and A_3 alone were present. A_2 is thus a 'negative cause', or preventive measure; if it acted alone, it would offset the effect of A_3. But in fact it did not act alone, it was itself offset by A_1.

It will be noticed that at least three causes must be at work for this to happen. In the case of a single cause, there is just one change of sign, from not-A ($-$) to A ($+$). In the case of two causes, if they are applied consecutively, there can still be no more than one change of sign ($--+$) or ($-++$). But in the case of three causes, there can be two changes of sign ($-+-+$). The second cause is then 'negative'[1].

If we think of B as a disaster, this is readily understandable. A_3 is the 'ultimate' cause. A_2 is a preventive measure, which if taken alone would have prevented the disaster. A_1 is a complication (or interference with the preventive measure) which prevents the prevention. So the disaster occurs. (In the causes of wars, and of strikes, and indeed in the medical field, one can readily find examples.) There can surely be no question that this is a configuration of which we have to take account.

Case (7) is just the same as case (6), save that here it is A_1 that is the negative cause. In case (8) both A_1 and A_2 are negative causes. It is asserted that either, if taken alone, would have been effective as prevention; but being taken together they interfere with one another and so the disaster occurs. This is of course a much more special case; but it could happen.

Every one of our eight cases has thus been accounted for ; an interpretation, an apparently quite reasonable interpretation, has been found for each. But there is something about the latter interpretations which does not satisfy.

---

[1] The economist will notice the analogy with his Production Function; if there are only two factors, they must be complements, but if there are three, one pair may be substitutes. Perhaps it is more than an analogy; both may be cases of a logical uniformity which is basically the same.

Our table was based on the supposition that A_1 and A_2 (and later A_3) were separable causes; but in the interpretation that has just been given for cases (6) to (8) has not that been abandoned? If (say) A_2 and A_3 are separable causes, it must be conceivable that one could occur without the other; but how can there be a prevention if there is nothing to prevent? If A_2 is a measure that was taken to offset the (direct) effect of A_3, A_3 is itself one of the causes of A_2; if not-A_3, then not-A_2. So we cannot complete our analysis of these more complicated cases without paying attention to the properties of non-separable causes.[2]

There is one case of non-separable causes which is very generally recognized. We may assert that A and A* are both causes of B, yet we do not believe it to be possible that one could occur without the other. If not-A, then not-A*; if not-A*, then not-A. We cannot then distinguish between them by considering a not-A, in which A* is present, or a not-A*, in which A is present; for neither of these alternatives can be constructed. The only alternative involving them which can be constructed is that in which neither is present.

Is such a relation, between A and A*, a causal relation? It is very like a causal relation, since it states that not-A implies not-A*; it seems to be a causal relation both ways. If, however, we hold to Hume's principle, that cause precedes effect, it cannot be a causal relation; for if it were, A would have to precede A*, and A* precede A; and that is impossible. However, it was recognized, indeed by Kant himself, that

---

[2] It is not to be denied that it is possible for a negative cause to be separable; it could have offset the original cause, without being caused by it. But the interesting cases of negative causes arise when they are (attempted) preventions; and these must be caused by the original.

there is an analogy between such a relation and that of causality. In the English translation of his *Critique*, the relation is called *reciprocity*; but his German word was *Wechselwirkung*; the literal translation of that is *mutual causality*. It would indeed seem logical to accept that mutual causality is a kind of causality; and if one accepts that effect cannot come before cause, it is a kind of causality that must be *contemporaneous*.

That, then, is one kind of non-separability; but is it the only kind? It does not fit our case of the prevention; for in that case there was a causal relation between the causes, but it was a causal relation that went only one way. Why not? The preventive measure could not have been taken if the original cause had not been present; the original cause might have been present yet the preventive measure might not have been taken. Some of the entries in a complete three-cause table (not shown) would therefore have been blank; just as, in the case of mutual causation between A_1 and A_2, not-A_1 alone and not-A_2 alone would have been blank. It does not seem to make much difference.

Nevertheless, if one holds to Hume's principle, there is a difference. For if it is always true that cause precedes effect, A_3 (as cause of A_2) must precede A_2; so A_1, A_2, A_3, as causes of B, are not contemporaneous. It will, however, be remembered that we began by asserting that B occurred at time T_b while its causes occurred at time T_a, so each cause occurred at the same time as the others. It now appears that this has to be waived; if so, it is rather serious.

We are indeed accustomed, especially in historical examples, to admit that an event may have causes that are differently dated. His naval defeat at Trafalgar (1805) and failure at Moscow (1812) were both causes of the fall of Napoleon (1814). Why not? We have ourselves, at an earlier stage in the present argument, when discussing overlapping causes, allowed that causes might be differently dated; and as we shall see, when the causes are separable, that is fairly harmless. But when the causes are non-separable, it is not so harmless; it has an important consequence, which needs to be noted.

The effect of the earlier cause (Trafalgar) comes after the later cause (Moscow). But if it is to have its effect at this later date, it must have some representative at the Moscow date, for time is continuous. So we have to suppose that it can be carried forward, so as to give it, in its 'later' capacity, a different date to that which it had in its 'earlier'. It would be the British sea-power, which was established at Trafalgar, which (on this arrangement) would be a cause of the fall of Napoleon; and that was a cause which continued after 1805, being still effective in 1812. The British sea-power and the failure at Moscow were contemporaneous causes. If they had been separable causes, that would give no trouble; they would just be additive, our case (1). But suppose that we assert that they were not separable. The Continental System, established by Napoleon, was a reply to the British blockade; and the Continental System, in its turn, was a cause of his quarrel with the Tsar. So Trafalgar, on this line of thought, was one of the causes of the failure at Moscow; 1805 and 1812 are sequential, there is no doubt about that. But if we bring the Trafalgar battle forward, representing it by the British sea-power, which was still effective in 1812, then (among the causes operating in 1812) there are two, one of which is the cause of the other. This is not mutual causation, which (as we have seen) can be dealt with by taking the two causes together. It is one-way causation, which nevertheless operates among contemporaneous causes.

I can see no way by which this is to be avoided; but why should we wish to avoid it? The obvious reason why so many (from Hume onwards) have wished to avoid it is that they have thought of the cause and the effect as operating, each, at a moment of time. If each is to occur at the same identical moment, there seems to be no time for the cause to 'take action'. This is partly a hang-over from what I have called the Old Causality; but it is not chiefly on that account that it has to be resisted.[3] As I began by indicating, T_a and T_b do not have to be moments; they can be periods, even quite long periods. When they are so interpreted, there is no reason why they should not be the same. There is plenty of time, over a period, for a cause to 'take effect'.[4]

I am not at all denying that there are many causal relations which are sequential, effect coming after cause; nor that there are many contemporaneous relations which are reciprocal or mutual, each of the elements being a cause of the other. I am simply asserting that there are many such relations which are contemporaneous but not reciprocal. In economics, we shall

---

[3] In view of its concern with the making of decisions, and with their consequences, there is more than a trace of the Old Causality which survives in economics. (See below, Chapter VII.)

[4] It may also be objected that if A and B are contemporaneous, B must be one of the *other things* which remain unchanged in not-A; so 'not-A implies not-B' is impossible. It will however be remembered that we did not define not-A as including all events, other than A, occurring at time T_a, but only 'all other potential separable causes'. How these should be identified is a matter of theory, of the theory which we are using. There is nothing illogical in having a theory in which B is not a potential cause—of itself! I shall be returning to this question of identification in Chapter III.

see, they are particularly important; but it is not only in economics that they arise.

I have insisted that the assertion 'if not-A, then not-B' is theoretical; it is derived from something which in the most general sense may be described as a theory, or model. It is by no means necessary that a theoretical relation, between contemporaneous events (that is to say, between possible contemporaneous events) should be reciprocal; in most of our economic models we have some relations which are reciprocal, but some which are not. We do indeed have a name for elements which can only enter into what, from the point of view of the theory, are non-reciprocal relations; we call them *exogenous*. From the point of view of the theory, an exogenous element (or the taking of some particular value by an exogenous element) cannot be an effect. It can only be a cause.

It must indeed be conceded that the abundance of exogenous elements in economics is no cause for congratulation; it is an indication of the modesty of the scientific status, if indeed it is a scientific status, which is all that economics can hope to achieve. It is because the range of phenomena with which economics deals is so narrow that economists are so continually butting their heads against its boundaries. If there were such a thing as an inclusive human science—a Sociology in Herbert Spencer's sense—it might not so often be butting against its boundaries; there might be few things which were relevant to it and yet were exogenous to it. But there are so many things which are relevant to economics and which yet are exogenous to it.

This is not the only way in which a science may have to take account of exogenous elements, however. It can happen, even in the natural sciences, that a new factor is introduced into the analysis of a situation, a factor that had previously been omitted. Even though the new factor is similar in character to those already allowed for, so that its introduction oversteps no boundary, nevertheless at the moment of its introduction it is (temporarily) exogenous. It is exogenous to the theory (or model) that previously existed. This can happen even when the new factor is a contemporaneous cause.

A most instructive example of this (far away from economics, but so instructive that it will be useful to give it a moment's attention) is the famous story of the discovery of the planet Neptune, one of the most spectacular achievements of Newtonian mechanics. The existence of Neptune was deduced, by Adams and Le Verrier, from the discrepancies that had for some years been observed between the actual path of the nearest interior planet (Uranus) and the path that had been calculated for it by astronomers, in which all known sources of perturbation had already been taken into account. And their deduction was verified. One may formally say that from the standpoint of the previously existing model, Neptune was an exogenous element; but the significance of the story goes deeper than that. It has a temporal aspect, not so often noticed.[5]

Uranus was discovered in 1781; Neptune was discovered in 1846. Now it so chanced that in 1823 the two planets were in conjunction (the distance between them was at a minimum); so it was precisely over the period to which the observations in question referred that the gravitational pull of Neptune on Uranus was at its maximum. Since the orbital period of Uranus is 68 years and that of Neptune 165 years, it is only now,

---

[5] I owe the facts used above to the fascinating analysis of the Neptune story that is given in R. A. Lyttleton, *Mysteries of the Solar System* (OUP 1968) ch. 7.

in the last quarter of the twentieth century, that the phenomenon will be repeated. If the discovery of Uranus had been eighty years later, the two planets would have been on opposite sides of the sun, and it would have been many years before a perturbation could have been detected.

The significant thing about this story, for my present purpose, is that it would have been quite fair to say, *after* the discovery, that the near approach of Neptune, during the period 1800–1840, had been shown to be the *cause* of the disturbance in the path of Uranus, *during that same period*. Contemporaneous causation! Contemporaneous causation that extended over a long period, in this case quite forty years.

Contemporaneous causation, as it appears in economics, does not usually extend over periods as long as that; we commonly confine it to much shorter periods, as for instance a year. Economics is largely concerned with 'flow' magnitudes, what is produced, or consumed, or paid over, during such a period. The relations between such magnitudes may be reciprocal (or mutual); but we often find ourselves treating one as exogenous, others as consequences; the one therefore as cause, the others as effects. I shall be examining some of these, in detail, in Chapters 5 and 6 below.

We have however seen, from the Neptune example, that the period of contemporaneous causation may be long; can it be extended indefinitely? Modern physicists are bold enough to fix a date for the origin of the universe—and a much nearer date, but itself in the distant future, when the earth will become uninhabitable; so if one speaks of indefinite duration, it cannot be duration on that time-scale. It can only be extension within some field of relevance. Yet one can again go to physics for an example.

It makes sense to say that the attraction of the moon is the cause of the tides. More precisely, it is the fact that the month (the orbital period of the moon round the Earth) is longer than the day (the period of the Earth's rotation) which is the cause of the tides. Now astronomers tell us that a time will come, at a vast but not incalculable distance in the future, when the action of the tides will so slow down the Earth's rotation that day and month will come together; and then there will be not tides in the seas any more. This information is interesting, but for human affairs it is irrelevant. In economics, as indeed in all other human studies (even in biology) it does not concern us. Our business is with a small segment of the astronomer's time, and over that segment the length of the day and the length of the (lunar) month can be taken as fixed. So, over that segment, their inequality *is* the cause of the tides. This is contemporaneous causation, though it goes on, so far as we are concerned, forever. Its period is of indefinite duration.

It would accordingly appear, from this example, that there is, after all, a kind of causality which is out of time. There can be causal relations which, so far as we are concerned, can be regarded as permanencies. This *static* causality (as with an eye to the economic examples, to which we shall be coming, it will be quite proper to call it) may indeed be regarded as a limiting case of contemporaneous causality—a contemporaneous causality in which the period, during which the cause operates and takes effect, has been so stretched out to become indefinite. I would yet maintain that when we proceed to this limit, there is a change of character. It is like the change familiar to economists, between the 'short period' and the 'long period' of Marshall. Short-period effects are in time, since they relate to what happens in a period, which begins from a point at which the fixed capital stock, of the firm or of the economy, has the particular form which it has at some particular date. Long-period effects are not in that way in time; for the long period has no clear beginning and no clear end. Much more will be said on this matter in the chapters that follow. It will suffice, for the present, to have shown by this Marshallian parallel, that the distinction is one which, at least in economics, is important. I am nevertheless presenting it in more general terms, since I want to contend that it is not only in economics that we need it.

The classification that has been elaborated in this chapter is quite complex; but when we look it over, from the point now reached, its shape becomes clear. Our rejection of Hume's principle, that cause *necessarily* precedes effect, has made it clearer. We have distinguished three kinds of causality, in relation to time: sequential (in which cause precedes effect), contemporaneous (in which both relate to the same time-period) and static (in which both are permanencies). The logical classification, with which we began, can be interpreted in any of these temporal senses. Even static causality may be strong or weak; it may be additive or overlapping; negative causes are not ruled out. It may be one-way, or it may be mutual. But it is always true that any statement of causality, of whatever kind, has reference to a theory; it is because we regard the events, which we state to be causally related, as instances of a theory, that we can make the statement of relation between them. So all statements of causality are matters of application of theory; but what is theory? That is the question which will be examined in the chapter that follows.

III
Theory and Application

Causality, of whatever kind, is always a relation, a relation between facts. And yet it appears to be a theoretical relation. How can there be a theoretical relation between facts? This is a paradox which has long troubled philosophers; it would be rash to claim that one can resolve it. We may nevertheless find the beginnings of a resolution by looking at the precise form of the theoretical statement we have been using: if not-A, then not-B. It has already become clear that we do not include in not-A all conceivable things other than A, and in not-B all conceivable things other than B; a theoretical relation between classes that are as wide as that must be impossible, or meaningless. What we have to include in not-A and not-B are relevant alternatives. Thus we have one class consisting of A and relevant alternatives to A, and another consisting of B and relevant alternatives to B. A has a characteristic a which the alternatives to it do not have, B a characteristic β which the alternatives to it do not have. Not-a and not-β are the characteristics of the remaining members. What the theory has to give us is a rule of implication. Not-a implies not-β.

Even so, we are back with the former paradox; how can one characteristic imply another? Implication is naturally taken to be a relation between propositions;

a characteristic is not a proposition. One cannot deduce one characteristic from another, as in mathematics one deduces a proposition from a set of axioms. (An axiom, of course, is itself a proposition; it is just a proposition from which one starts.) Accordingly, before deduction can get to work, it needs something more than the recognition of a characteristic. It has to begin from some proposition, some relation between characteristics that has already been recognized, and that cannot be provided by deduction. It follows that if a theory is to be applied to facts (if it is not a *pure* theory, which is at liberty to choose its own axioms) it must begin from some proposition, or propositions, which are not deductive in origin but inductive. Though (as we shall see) deduction has a part to play, the theories on which the assertion of causal relations must be based cannot be purely deductive.

Can they be purely inductive? It has often been supposed (from Hume onwards) that they can be, indeed that they must be. When we assert that one characteristic implies another, we are not using the word 'imply' in a logical, or mathematical sense. We are merely asserting that as a matter of observation, the two are found together.

If one takes this view, the relation between the characteristics is purely empirical. We do indeed have plenty of examples of empirical relations (there are many, as we shall be seeing, in economics); they have been elaborately studied, on their own account, and ways of dealing with them have been continually improved. It rarely happens that there is a perfect concordance. When the characteristics are measured in quantitative terms, as usually happens, there is not a perfect correlation. How much faith should be given to an imperfect correlation, a partial, but not complete, measure of agreement? Ways of estimating the confidence which should be given to imperfect correlation, and similar imperfect fits, are now well known; but it is assumed in these estimates that if we found a perfect fit, over an indefinitely large number of instances, we should have perfect confidence in it. It is granted that in practice the number of instances that can be presented is finite, not indefinitely large; so that we can never have a quite perfect confidence. But if the number of instances is large, we are supposed to have a near-perfect confidence; it is assumed that we should then be persuaded that in instances not so far presented the 'law' would still hold. But should we be so persuaded? I believe that in general one does ask for more.

The two have, in our experience, been found together; one still asks—why? The empirical association still lacks a reason. But that again brings us to the paradox; for when we demand a reason we are asking that the empirical association should be brought into a logical system. We are asking that the two senses of implication, empirical and logical, should be brought together.

Can that be done? There is plenty of experience, in science (and even in economics) to show that it can. For the statement of association, though it is itself of purely inductive character, is nevertheless a proposition; in that capacity, as a proposition, it can have implications, in the logical sense. Some of these implications may be testable, inductively; in important cases they are testable. If the test is successful, a bridge, a logical bridge, has been built between two inductions; the coherence, the logical coherence, of the bridge strengthens our confidence in the inductions which are its supports.

Science has many examples of this; it will be useful to set out one of them. I shall take what is surely a leading example. When Newton discovered gravitation, he took the first big step towards the creation of modern science. There can be no more important example to take.

How did Newton make his discovery? The apple that fell from a tree is obvious mythology; where Newton started must have been further on than that. He must surely have been acquainted, directly or indirectly, with the work of Galileo on projectiles (Galileo had died in the year that Newton was born). It had already been shown by Galileo that the path of a projectile can be analysed as having a horizontal component, which (his experiments seemed to show) would exhibit constant velocity, and a vertical component, with acceleration *downwards*. All that had been shown by Galileo, *inductively*. It was an easy next step to observe that the same is true at different places on the surface of the (spherical) Earth; so the evidence is that the acceleration is directed towards the centre of the Earth. At that point the mathematician takes over. What can be said, in general, about the motion of a body that is moving with an acceleration directed towards a fixed point? If it starts from rest, it will just fall towards that point, like the apple; but if, like the projectile, it has another independent motion, that does not follow. What does follow (and it needed no more than a very little calculus, well within the capacity of even the early Newton, to show it) is that, whatever be the 'law' of the acceleration, the path must lie in a plane, and must exhibit what is now called constancy of angular momentum—'equal areas in equal times'. Kepler's Second Law of planetary motion! These laws had been established by Kepler, half a century before Newton, *purely inductively*; taking the observations of planetary movements, which had been made for centuries, re-arranging them in Copernican terms, and then looking for uniformities. When Newton had shown that this second of Kepler's laws would also be true for a projectile, moving freely, it was natural to ask whether the others (the first and the third) would not also be true. If that could be shown it would follow that the planets were behaving like projectiles—which is precisely what the theory of gravitation maintains. So the mathematician could again get to work, this time working back from Kepler; and it turned out that the other laws would be verified (not just one but both of the other laws would be verified) on the single assumption that the law of force, the acceleration towards the centre, was proportional to the inverse square of the distance. The outline[1] of Newton's theory was then complete. Its validity was of course confirmed by further observations; but even with the (inductive) evidence already available to Newton, its persuasiveness was very great. For it had established a logical connection between inductions that had previously appeared to be quite independent. The coherence of the whole structure strengthened confidence in each of its parts.

Newton, in the last pages of *Principia*, insisted that his inverse-square law was not a hypothesis: 'hypotheses non fingo'. That is to say, it was not a hypothesis that had been introduced from outside, by some 'revelation' or stroke of genius; it was a relation that had emerged from the facts. Ultimately, therefore, it was founded on observations, on inductions. Yet it was considered (and Newton himself considered it) to be a relation that had been *proved*. But can a law be *proved* by inductions? Though the number of observations was large, it was still finite; no piling-up of observations can ever achieve complete proof. What gave the Newtonian theory its strength was not only the number of observations that were

---

[1] Of course it was only in outline that it was complete. There was much more to be done before Newton himself was satisfied.

consistent with it, but also that by its logic it indicated ways of making new observations, different kinds of new observation, which for long continued to confirm it, so that its inductive strength continually increased. That is probably the nearest thing to 'proof' which any theory, or general statement, which is to apply to reality, can ever have.

Within the range of observation that was possible for Newton (and even much further) nothing has ever been found that is inconsistent with his theory; nothing at all was found for two centuries after Newton's date. Only in the last hundred years, when distances (and velocities) that had previously been unmeasurable became measurable, did the qualifications (especially associated with Einstein) have to be introduced. Even now, within the range of phenomena that was accessible to Newton, the qualifications are unimportant. The Newtonian theory still stands, within its own field of reference. That is as much as has ever been achieved by any scientific theory.

Further, within its own field, the Newtonian theory is remarkably complete. Within the range of phenomena to which it applies, it establishes *strong* causal connections; its laws are valid, with a minimum of 'other things being equal'. There is no reason why we should expect this to hold at all generally. Weak causality, as we have seen, is the more general case. A law which establishes no more than weak causality, indicating no more than one of the causes at work, can still be very useful. And so can a law that is based on inductions which are less firm than Newton's were. Though Newton's is a supreme example of a scientific theory, it is also an extreme example.

The pattern of deductions serving as a bridge between inductions is, however, general. The chain of deduction may be short or long, simple or complex.

When it is simple, we can usually detect some primary observations, from which deductions are made; the deductions then indicate what secondary observations, or experiments, should be made to seek for confirmation. The secondary observations *verify* the theory.

Nevertheless, as the Newtonian example makes clear, this simple order is not necessary. If we call Galileo's observations primary and Kepler's secondary (as they appeared to be in the way I presented the story), both had been made before, indeed long before, Newton came on the scene. Here, in order that the bridge should be built, what was needed was a mathematical development, the invention of the calculus, which had not been made in the days of Kepler or of Galileo. When science has advanced to a point where it needs a development in mathematics, not yet made, the further advance has to wait for the mathematical development. There would seem to be several examples of this in modern physics—wave mechanics, relativity, quantum mechanics and so on. It is a sequence which is quite likely to occur when the mathematical demands are great.

One can easily see, from this point of view, why it is that the discovery of a fact (or observation), which is inconsistent with an established theory, does not always cause that theory to be abandoned, or not at least to be abandoned straightaway. There are several examples of this in the history of science; to some thinkers about the history of science they have been thought to be upsetting.[2] But if the former theory had

---

[2] Much attention has been given to this matter by methodologists, especially by those of the school of Imre Lakatos. (See the volumes on *Method and Appraisal*, edited by Howson and Latsis, which report the proceedings of a conference, held in 1974 at Nafplion in Greece, at which I had the advantage of being present.)

been properly[3] established, it must have been based on some evidence; all that can then be shown by the new evidence is that its field of application is narrower than had been thought. That is no reason for abandoning it within its now more limited field; not at least until a new theory has been developed, with a wider field of application. When the latter requires new concepts, and new methods, especially mathematical methods, the development of the new theory may take a good deal of time. It is foolish to abandon what we have already got until we have something better, or wider.

Let us however return to the easier case, where the chain of deduction is fairly short, so that the logical order, from primary observations, through deductions, to secondary observations, is also the temporal order. Once a theory, or stage in a theory, has been established on this basis—when it has been confirmed by its secondary observations—these, in their turn, may be used as primary observations for a further stage. If this procedure is followed, the stages of the theory are like rungs on a ladder; the investigator climbs from one to the next. It will be useful to have this image in mind, though it is over-simplified; for the primary observations that are employed at each stage of a theory do not necessarily come from the same sequence of discovery. There is cross-fertilization between different sequences. We nevertheless find that there are some sequences which belong together, so that the primary observations that are used in each stage of each come from other sequences which are of

---

[3] There have indeed been important pseudo-scientific theories, 'hypotheses' in Newton's sense, which have attracted adherents, even though they were based on hardly any empirical evidence. And there have been others, for which there appeared to be evidence, but the evidence has not stood up to criticism.

the same 'family'. Such families of sequences are regarded as constituting a (particular) science. But even between sciences there may be cross-fertilization.[4]

With this understanding the image of the ladder will not do too badly as a representation of the progress of a particular science. But where does the ladder start? What are the primary observations from which the sequence begins? They cannot be secondary observations coming from some former rung, for there is no former rung. They are pure inductions, which are not verifications of some hypothesis,[5] derived from results which have been already obtained. How is it possible to make such pure inductions?

The Baconian heresy, that such inductions can be obtained by mere collection of facts, without ordering principle, has long been rejected by scientists; in the light of what was said at the beginning of this chapter, we can see why. A statement that two characteristics are commonly found together, which is the simplest form of a primitive induction, already requires that a class of phenomena (objects or events) should have been distinguished—the phenomena which have the characteristics in question. So there is a work of *classification* which has to be performed before the inductions can be made. It is a work which from one point of view is external to the science in which the inductions will be used; for it is a work which must be performed

---

[4] So some instances of arrest in the development of a science may be explained, not by waiting until the required mathematics has been developed (as in the examples from physics previously noted) but by waiting until some other science has been developed, the results of which are required for further advance in the first. An instance which comes to mind is the lag in biology, during much of the nineteenth century; it was waiting for Genetics.

[5] In the ordinary sense of *hypothesis*, not in Newton's.

before the 'climbing' can start. But from another point of view it is the first stage of the science; when the history of the science comes to be written, it is from these preliminary classifications that its story will begin.

When these classifications are first formed, the science is still in the future; so we should not be surprised to find that as they start they are unscientific. Their purpose, at that stage, is not the advancement of science; it is something quite different. The primitive classifications which led to astronomy were made, in the first place, by astrologers; it was the (mistaken) belief that human events were governed by the stars which provided the first incentive to the collection, and classification, of astronomical facts. There is a somewhat similar relation of alchemy to chemistry. But it is probable that chemistry owes more to the inductive knowledge that was built up, from very early times, by technicians, such as metal-workers. In a similar way the medical sciences begin with empiricists ('quacks'). One of the chief sources of primitive inductions is the practical arts.

Even during this preliminary phase, it was possible to make progress. Classifications could be improved. It is indeed not easy to say what, at that stage, would be the canon of improvement. Looking back, we can reckon a classification as better if it led to inductions that were more fertile, so that they could be used as primitive inductions for a (later) 'ladder' of development. But this could not be perceived at the date in question. All that could (perhaps) be perceived would be a gain in simplicity.

We can find an example at a corresponding stage of the story we have been using. The Copernican revolution, in itself, was no more than an improvement in classification. Instead of reckoning the sun as a planet, and the earth as something different, Copernicus proposed to regard the sun as something different and the earth as a planet. Taken by itself this did not have much persuasive power, and we know that for many years not much attention was paid to it. Only when Kepler, by his enormous calculations, showed that inductive laws could be formulated in terms of Copernicus, but not in terms of Ptolemy; and when Galileo, by his discovery of the moons of Jupiter, found new phenomena which fitted into the Copernican classification; only then did Copernicus win general acceptance. But we are then at the beginning of science in the narrower sense.

How does all this apply to economics? The preliminary phase, in the case of economics, is readily recognizable. Just as the first steps towards the natural sciences were made by non-scientists, so the first steps towards economics were made by non-economists. Administrators, calculating imports and exports; accountants, calculating profits and incomes and drawing up balance-sheets; it is from the work of such practical people that economics begins. And just as in the natural sciences, the first step towards science proper is the refinement of unscientific, or semi-scientific, classifications, so there is in economics a corresponding proceeding, the refinement of the practical concepts so as to fit them better to be tools of thinking. In economics it is a major activity. It leads to social accounting, and to the critique of social accounting; the search for concepts (or classifications) which will facilitate an intelligible *description* of economic facts. We do indeed speak of descriptive economics; economics which describes, but does not attempt to explain.

The scientist explains by means of his 'ladder'; but where in economics is the 'ladder', the regular progression from one established induction to another? We have hardly more than fragments of it; and the reason is evident. It is just that economics is in time, in a way that the natural sciences are not. All economic data are dated; so that inductive evidence can never do more than establish a relation which appears to hold within the period to which the data refer. If a relation has held, with no more than intelligible exceptions, over (say) the last fifty years, we may reasonably guess that it will continue to hold this year, and perhaps next year, and perhaps for the year after that. But we cannot even reasonably guess that it will continue to hold for the next fifty years. In the sciences such guesses are reasonable; in economics they are not.

Economics, as I said, is on the edge of science and on the edge of history. Some further consequences of this peculiar status will be explored in the following chapters.

IV
'Statics' and 'equilibrium'

One aspect of the difference between the sciences and economics has yet to be noted. The sciences are full of measurements which, over a wide field of application, can be regarded as constants—the absolute zero of temperature is –273° centigrade, the number of chromosomes in the human zygote is forty-six, and so on—but there are no such constants in economics. There are indeed some price-ratios which for long periods have been fixed by law, such as the gold value of the pound sterling between 1821 and 1914; but to the economist these are 'artificial' and clearly exceptional. Again, there have been some apparent constants, or near-constants, such as the nine- or ten-year length of the Trade Cycle, which for roundabout half a century, between 1820 and 1870, appeared to have become established (so established, indeed, that Jevons dared to associate it with the sunspot cycle, thus reducing it into strictly physical terms); but *regular* fluctuation, on this pattern, has not persisted. The economic world, it has in our day become increasingly obvious, is inherently in a state of flux.

Economists, nevertheless, seek to imitate the scientists; and when they do so they are inevitably drawn to a study of the nearest approximations to constancy which their subject permits, to a study of those relations which appear to be fairly persistent, so they can be taken, over long periods, to remain more or less unchanged. The nearest parallels, in economics, to physical theories must therefore be found in *static* theories. Not static theories of the text-book variety, which are admitted to require much adaptation before they can be applied to reality; but static theories which do have reference, direct reference, to facts. These are not very common; it is easier to find them if we go back to the beginnings of economics, to theories which were developed to deal with economic affairs which were not changing so incessantly as they change now. So it will not be inappropriate to take a historical example, from Adam Smith. It will be useful to see how far we can fit it into the pattern that has been described. Can we reduce it to the form of the 'bridge', deduction bridging inductions?

The argument may be set out as follows. It begins, as the *Wealth of Nations* itself begins, with the division of labour (specialization); a major source, as Smith continually maintained, of improvement in productivity. But 'the division of labour is limited by the extent of the market'.[1] (It was for this reason that he so strongly opposed mercantilism; for 'artificial' restraints on trade diminished the extent of the market. But that is not the direction in which I want to follow him here.)

He knew that artificial restrictions did no more than aggravate the natural restrictions, due to costs of transport, so much more formidable in his day than they have become in ours. He was also aware that transport by water was, again in his day, in general much cheaper than transport by land. 'Live cattle are perhaps the only commodity of which the transport is

---

[1] Wealth of Nations (Oxford edition, 1976) p. 31.

more expensive by sea than by land.'[2] It clearly follows, from these two considerations taken together, that places with easy access to water transport should have a locational advantage. 'As by means of water-carriage a more extensive market is opened to every sort of industry than what land-carriage alone can afford it, so it is upon the sea-coast, and along the banks of navigable rivers, that industry of every kind naturally begins to sub-divide and improve itself.'[3] And that should lead to such places becoming richer than their neighbours—and Smith, looking around him, could assure himself that they (at least quite frequently) did.

This is the argument (a very simple argument) which I shall proceed to examine. It will be noticed that in spite of its dependence on the 'law of increasing returns', which fits so badly into modern static models, it is nevertheless in our sense static. The conditions to which it refers are such as appeared, in Smith's day, to be permanent. Even the relation between the costs of land and water transport was a fact which appeared in Smith's day to be permanent; it did in fact remain, much as it was, for long after his time. In our time it has changed. First by the railway, and then with road transport by motor vehicles, the costs of transporting goods by land have been drastically reduced—it can hardly be doubted that they have been relatively reduced. It is no longer the case that 'live cattle' are the only goods where land transport has an advantage; the range of goods for which land transport is cheaper has become far wider. The locational advantage of continental areas has accordingly increased, or their

---

[2] Ibid. p. 459. If cattle are taken by sea they have to be fed, but if they are taken by land they can feed themselves on the way!

[3] Ibid. p. 32.

disadvantage diminished. May not one of the
causes of the changes in relative wealth, which
have lately become so noticeable, have been this
change in relative costs? That is a question which
Smith, if confronted with our facts, would surely have
asked.

Let us now divide up the argument. One can distinguish five steps. The first is the statement of economies of specialization. As it appears in Smith, this is
clearly a matter of observation; it is not a logical
necessity. He does not need it as a necessity; only in
the form of an observation that there are many kinds
of production where large scale is more efficient.
That these were already, in his day, of considerable
importance could be no more than an empirical
fact.

The second is the relative cheapness of water
transport, to which the same, even more obviously,
applies. Both of these, then, are empirical observations.

The third, however, is a deduction. If the first two
steps are granted, the locational advantage of places
with good water connections *follows*.

The fourth is the step from locational advantage to
relative wealth. This looks obvious, but we shall find it
to be crucial. Postponing it for a moment, let us pass
on to the fifth, which (on the pattern that has been
suggested) should be the confrontation of the effect,
which has been deduced, with experience. Do we in
fact find that places with good water connections are
richer? Were they richer, that is to say, in the time of
Smith? He could not have hoped to find such perfect
concordance as Newton found with the observations
of Kepler; all he could have hoped to produce would
have been some favourable evidence. London? Ham-
burg? Philadelphia? But he could hardly have failed to
notice exceptions. He could not therefore have pre-

tended that he had done any more than identify one of the causes of relative wealth.[4]

But let us go back to the fourth step—relative advantage *implies* relative wealth. This is a step which Smith often takes, not only in this context but in many others. It is so commonly taken, not only by Smith, but by most of his successors, that we shall need a name for it. I shall call it the *Economic Principle*. (It is much wider than the Profit Motive.)

How is this principle to be justified? One can regard it, like the first two steps, as being empirical. One can say that the economies with which Smith was dealing were such as to exhibit it; people would act *economically*; when the opportunity of an advantage was presented to them, they would take it. The people of Britain, of Holland and of America, about whom he was largely thinking, did seem to behave like that. And it should be noticed that if the gain was to be

---

[4] A striking exception, already remarkable in the time of Smith, was Geneva. The Rhone was not navigable for many miles below Geneva, but the wealth of Geneva was already outstanding. The musical traveller, arriving in Geneva in 1770, after crossing France, wrote as follows: 'I am in love with this place. I have eat, drank and slept, more comfortably than since I left England. Cleanliness, industry and plenty appear wherever I turn my eyes. All the way from Lyons the people were half-naked, hungry and wretched. But here no beggars, or barefooted people are seen on the streets.' (Dr. Charles Burney's Musical Tours, ed. Scholes, Oxford 1959, Vol. I, p. 41.) The explanation, of course, was that Geneva had specialized upon the production of watches, a commodity of high value in relation to bulk, so that cost of transport, even by land, was an unusually small proportion of the total price to the final purchaser. The facility of water transport, along the lake of Geneva, cannot have been more than a minor factor.

perceptible (to an observer) it would not be sufficient that just here and there the opportunity was taken; it would have to be taken on a sufficient scale. Can that be other than an empirical observation?

Many later commentators have concluded that that is what it is. Smith is simply describing what he sees around him, the particular stage which 'capitalism' has reached in his time. But it is not necessary to take him that way, nor (in view of the importance which he attaches to the Principle) is it natural to take him that way. If an economy is sluggish, so that when an opportunity comes, no more than a small part of it is taken, the rest will still be there, for others to take. So, even in a sluggish economy, the time should come when others follow; in time the reaction will spread and so become 'sufficient'. If this is not to happen (and if the opportunity is such that it continues to be open) there must be obstacles to the spreading. Smith was well aware of the importance of obstacles; he has much to say about them in many parts of his book. He would surely have agreed that the obstacles which are present at one place and time are not the same as those present at another place and time; so the application of the principle to different times and places is to that extent an empirical matter. But does this mean that the principle itself is similarly empirical? I cannot believe that Smith would have admitted that it is.

He would have a way out. He could maintain that the principle was one of definition, or classification. No one really denies that people *sometimes* act in pursuit of objectives, their own objectives. (It is now well-known that the eighteenth-century discussion of this in terms of self-interest was too narrow. I need not go into that.) What Smith is doing is to *define* that kind of action as economic action, while admitting that its 'free play' may be trammelled by obstacles. It is what his successors have been doing (with few—perhaps only apparent—exceptions) ever since. The list of obstacles which a modern economist would introduce would no doubt be different from Smith's; but the method is the same. We still find it useful to begin by inquiring what consequences will follow if opportunities are taken; and then to inquire, in a particular application, what obstacles there are in the way.

Even if it is granted that in the absence of obstacles, opportunities will be taken, the question remains; will they be taken quickly or slowly? It is possible to interpret a slowness of reaction as itself due to obstacles, and there are purposes for which that is useful; but in a static theory, to be used for the study of static causation, it is unlikely to be convenient. It is more convenient to use the *equilibrium method*.

Let us look back at the locational problem. Adam Smith, as we have seen, is saying that the relative cheapness of water transport is a cause of the relative wealth of some places that have good water communications. He is thus (in terms of our analysis of causation) comparing what was in his time with what *would have been* if, other things being equal, the relative costs of land and water carriage had been different. He must thus be thought of as constructing a theoretical model, in which relative costs are changed but other things are not changed. What was in his time is what was in his lifetime, or over the time his memory extends—quite a long period. The model must refer to the same period. But since it is only the things which in the actual experience remain, more or less, unchanged over time which are relevant to the comparison, it would seem to follow that the model itself must be unchanging. Change over time, within its period, cannot enter into it, since such change is irrelevant to it. That is the first sense in which the model must be in equilibrium.

But when the Economic Principle is applied to such

a model, it will follow that all opportunities for advantageous change that are presented within the model must within the model be taken. So in that second and deeper sense the model must be in equilibrium. The system of prices and incomes must be such that an equilibrium in which they rule is possible.

Can one however be sure that such an equilibrium would be attainable? It has become evident in later work that the Economic Principle by itself gives no guarantee that an equilibrium can be established. It has been shown that the class of models to which the Economic Principle can be applied is a very wide one (including, for instance, those which can be applied to political relations between states, or parties); anything which can be reduced to a 'game'. The study of the models which can be generated from the principle by the introduction of such axioms, or assumptions, as we please is a branch of mathematics. Though it was originally suggested by the economic application, it has in our day much outgrown it. It has been demonstrated, in this mathematics, that a model, to which the Economic Principle can be applied, does not have to have an equilibrium.

It has nevertheless been generally claimed by economists that their models, their static models, indeed especially their static models, do have an equilibrium; and in the simplest type of classical model it is clear that this is so. In that model the prices of products are shown to be determined by technical considerations, by the quantities of the factors of production (already identified as labour, capital and land) which are required to make a unit of each finished product. These technical coefficients, as they later came to be called, would determine the cost of production of each product, and the Economic Principle would keep prices equal to costs. They would be kept in equality by the opportunities for movement of capital and of labour from a less to a more advantageous line of production, which would be opened by any divergence. So if the technical coefficients had been different, the equilibrium would be changed, in a manner which could be deduced. Actual conditions, in an actual economy over a particular period, would not correspond exactly with the model, but there would be some configuration of coefficients which would be approximately actual; the model could then be used to show (again no doubt approximately, very approximately) how the system would have been modified if some of these exogenous elements, the technical coefficients, had been different. Causation, in the static sense, could thus for some problems (as for instance the locational problem with which we began) be established.

This reliance on technical coefficients—relations the reality of which could hardly be questioned, though they were imported from 'outside' economics—was a strength of this classical model. In the days of Adam Smith (less perhaps in the days of his successors, Ricardo and Mill) the techniques of production were not changing rapidly, so the technical coefficients could be regarded as rather *firm*. Notice, for instance, that in dealing with international trade, there was no question but that the labour required for the production of a particular commodity *is* greater in one country than in another. But the firmness of technical coefficients could not have helped them as much as it did, if it had not been for the long-period application from which, as has been suggested, the theory emerged.

The range of problems to which such a model could be applied was nevertheless limited. For in strictness it is only if there is just one original factor, into terms of which all costs are ultimately reducible (the 'labour theory of value') that the technical coefficients are sufficient to determine relative costs; if there is more than one factor, the relative prices of the factors may also play a part. So it is only for problems where changes in relative factor-prices can be neglected that it can be safe, even for long-period purposes, to use the simple model. That can indeed happen, for either of two reasons, Either the changes (between actuality and the hypothetical situation with which we are comparing it) are such that we judge it unlikely that they will have a significant effect upon relative factor prices; or it may be such that we judge it unlikely to have a significant effect upon the proportions in which the factors are combined, for in that case also the 'bundle' of factors may be treated as a single factor. If either of these conditions is satisfied—and experience has shown that cases in which we can rely upon one or other of them are not so uncommon[5]—the simple classical theory can be used, and has proved its worth. When we cannot use it, we get into deeper trouble.

It will be useful to sketch out some of the difficulties which then arise, and to classify the kinds of response which economists have made to them. They lead to different kinds of static analysis. Each has its limitations, but the limitations are different.

I begin with one which has associations with the work of Smith and Ricardo, though I shall state it in more modern terms. It is generated in the following way.

One first observes that if a model is to be static, unchanging over time, the supplies of the factors must be unchanging. So one might solve the factor-price problem by saying that these prices must be such as to keep the supplies of the factors from changing. It is not implausible to suppose that the prices of the factors have some influence on their supplies. Thus there should be some rate of 'wages' which will keep the supply of labour constant, and some rate of 'profit'

---

[5] See pp. 60–1 below.

which will keep the supply of capital constant. But why should these be consistent with one another? It is not obvious that they have to be consistent.

They can nevertheless be made consistent by a variation on the static model. Since it would be the ratios of prices which would be kept firm by the technical coefficients (so long as the ratios of factor-prices were themselves unchanging), much of the static character of the model could be retained even though the economy as a whole was expanding. Its price-structure could still be static, even though the quantities of factors used, and the quantities of products produced from them, were expanding, so long as they kept in step. We would just have to add to the static properties of the model its constant growth rate. The model would be in what is now called a steady state.

Consistency between the 'supply functions' of the factors could then be restored. Consider Figure 1. In this diagram growth rates (of labour and of capital) are measured on the horizontal axis, wage (per unit of labour) on the vertical. The wage is measured in terms of the product (which, in a steady state, consists of a

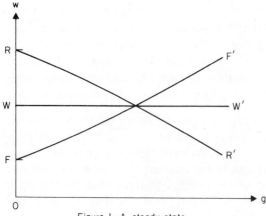

Figure 1 : A steady state

bundle of commodities combined in fixed proportions, so that it can be treated as a single product).
We suppose that there is some 'subsistence wage',
which is the minimum which must be given to labour
in order that the supply of labour should be maintained. It is marked at OF, on the vertical axis; thus if
the wage were no greater than OF, the growth rate of
labour supply would be zero, as shown. We could
similarly suppose that there would be some rate of
return to capital which would keep the supply of capital constant; that cannot be shown directly upon our
diagram, but it can be shown indirectly. For the higher
the wage, in terms of the product, the less is left over
for capital; there must thus be some wage which is so
high as to reduce the return on capital to its
minimum.[6] This wage can be shown on the diagram as
OR. As we saw, there is no reason why OR should be
equal to OF; it makes sense to suppose it greater than
OF. But if the supplies of both labour and capital are
to be kept constant, consistently, OR and OF must be
equal.

In an expanding economy, the dilemma is easily
resolved. If a wage that was equal to OF would keep
labour supply constant, a wage that was larger should
enable it to increase. Thus a 'supply curve' of labour,
in terms of growth rate, could be drawn as FF'; it
would slope upwards. By the device which has just
been explained, a 'supply curve' of capital (RR') could
be drawn on the same diagram. At a lower wage, with
more left over for capital, more would be available for

---

[6] Whether this minimum is to be taken as a positive rate of
return (as the Classical Economists usually thought it to
be) or whether it is a net return of zero, does not essentially
matter. It would surely be granted that capital could not
increase, if there were no other sources than profits from
which investment could be financed, and if gross profits did
not cover depreciation.

investment; so the supply of capital could increase. Thus RR' (on the diagram) should be downward–sloping.

Whatever the slopes of the curves, there must then be some rate of growth at which there will be intersection. At the corresponding level of wages (OW), the growth rates of labour and of capital would be the same, so that a steady state, of uniform expansion, would be possible. This equilibrium wage, it will be noticed, will be higher, the less extensible is the supply of labour, and the more extensible the supply of capital.

Such a model could readily be extended to admit a third factor, so long as that factor behaved in the same manner as those hitherto considered. There would then be three growth rates to be brought into equilibrium, but there would be two rates of 'wages' with which to do it. What one, as has been shown, could do for two, two could do for three. And so on.

The weakness of this model (as was, in effect, pointed out by Ricardo) lies in its assumption that the 'curves' RR' and FF' (or what would correspond to them in a three-factor model) can remain unchanged in a process of expansion. What is to happen if there is a factor (Ricardo's land) the supply of which has a *fixed* maximum, which is independent of the return which it gets? So long as that factor is not fully employed, the uniform expansion (as described) can persist, but at the point where it is fully employed, the expansion must stop. All that then is possible, if the assumptions hitherto made are retained, is a *stationary* equilibrium in which the supplies of all factors are constant and the outputs of all products are constant. But how, in that equilibrium, are the prices of the factors determined?

We have seen that in the uniform expansion the price of any factor would be higher the less extensible its supply; applying this principle to the present case, it would seem that in the stationary equilibrium, labour and capital would each be getting their minimum return, while land (the fixed factor) would swallow up the whole surplus. Such a stationary equilibrium is logically possible; but as a model to be used in the study of causality, it has not been generally found to be appealing.[7]

It was not what Ricardo himself had in mind. He did not make a sharp division between the two sorts of equilibrium—the uniform expansion in which land was not scarce and the stationary state in which land was fully employed. In his model the scarcity of land revealed itself gradually. There were *diminishing* returns to the application of labour and capital to land. This, in terms of our previous discussion, was an empirical observation, though one which was so 'obvious' that its truth could hardly be denied. Natural resources do set limits to possible expansion of output, but the limits are elastic. They can be overcome, to some extent, with sufficient trouble.

What then emerges may be illustrated in another diagram[8] (Figure 2). Here I still measure wages (in terms of product) along the vertical axis; but along the horizontal I now measure not growth rate but *quantity* of labour employed. OF and OR can still be marked

---

[7] For notice that if one held to a steady state model, as in fig 1, one would say that if the productivity of labour had been higher (so that the RR′ curve was raised) the wage would have been higher and the growth rate would have been higher; but if one held to a stationary state model, one would have to say that the only effect of a rise in productivity would be to raise rents.

[8] This is based on that which was used in the paper by Samuel Hollander and myself 'Mr. Ricardo and the Moderns' (QJE 1977). My collaborator in that paper has of course no responsibility for the use I am making of it here.

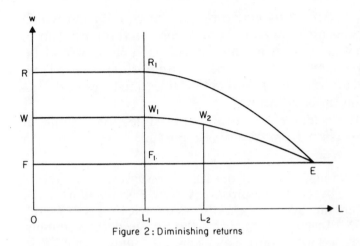

Figure 2: Diminishing returns

on the vertical axis, with their former meanings; save that OR now becomes the maximum that can be paid to labour, consistently with capital getting its minimum, *so long as land is not scarce*. Say that up to the point where labour supply is OL_1 land is not scarce. Then to the left of the vertical through L_1, the uniform expansion can proceed, with the wage at OW, as in the former diagram. The expansion can be represented by a movement to the right, along the line WW_1. There is a 'roof' at RR_1 and a 'floor' at FF_1, between which the wage must lie.

To the right of the vertical through L_1 the 'roof' slopes downwards. The shortage of land begins to reflect itself in the productivity of labour, so that the maximum wage which can be paid, consistently with capital getting its minimum, begins to fall. A point (E) must be reached, in the end, with floor and roof coming together; so the equilibrium wage, which must lie between this maximum and this minimum, becomes equal to each. A stationary state is reached at E.

The path of the economy, as represented by the wage, must therefore be somewhat as represented by

W_1E. An actual economy, or the equilibrium which represents it, must be somewhere on this path. But in what sense can a wage, which is such as would be represented by W_2L_2, be an equilibrium wage? How can an economy that is in that situation be regarded as being in equilibrium?

It is clearly not in a steady state, for a uniform expansion from W_2 is not possible.[9] Not is it in a

---

[9] An ingenious way out has been suggested in a recent paper by Carlo Casarosa ('A New Formulation of the Ricardian System', Oxford Economic Papers, March 1978.) Instead of supposing the roof to decline continuously, as I have drawn it on Figure 2, he supposes it to fall in steps. Thus at each step a uniform expansion would be (locally) possible; over a range the economy could still be in a steady state.

I fully admit that the model can be 'mended' in this way; but as an interpretation of Ricardo his model seems to me to be open to two objections. First, the 'steps' must be very long if the equilibrium thus attained can be more than a short-run equilibrium; and an equilibrium which is to be reached by adjustment of factor supplies could hardly be reached in less than a quite long time. In the second place, while it is understandable that land may be of various qualities, and that the supply of each quality of land may be large, a model which relies entirely upon this (as Casarosa's model does) must assume that the 'falls', from one 'step' to the next, are vertical; so that it is highly unlikely that the economy will be in a position which is intermediate between steps. I cannot believe that this was Ricardo's intention. For he himself says 'It . . . commonly happens that before . . . the inferior lands are cultivated, capital can be employed more productively on those lands which are already in cultivation' (Principles, Chapter on Rent, Vol. I of Sraffa edition, p. 71). This would seem to imply that the falls are gradual, so that an intermediate position, at which diminishing returns are clearly exhibited, is very likely to be actual.

stationary condition, for the supplies of both capital and labour, at W_2, are tending to increase. So it cannot be an equilibrium in either of the senses that we have considered hitherto. If it is to be an equilibrium, it must be an equilibrium in some other sense.[10]

So it is not surprising to find that later economists (the so-called neo-classics) had a static equilibrium which was different. Being less impressed than Ricardo by the population peril (and having learned by experience that growth in labour supply is a more complex matter than can be reduced to dependence upon a single variable)[11] they found it wiser to treat the supplies of the factors, not only labour but also capital, as exogenous variables. That is to say, they would be changeless over time, for the model would still be a static model; they would vary from one state of the model to another (the hypothetical states still

---

[10] It would be a distraction from my present purpose to enlarge upon the way in which (in my belief) Ricardo thought himself to have eluded the difficulty. It has been explained at length in the Hicks-Hollander paper previously cited. I believe that he began by thinking in terms of a purely circulating capital model, in which capital is simply 'advances to labourers'. In such a model the rate of real wages is determined by the volume of capital (the wage-fund) and by the condition (quite a short-run equilibrium condition) that the demand for labour should equal the supply. An equilibrium path, which satisfies that condition, can readily be constructed. It must lie between the floor and the roof (except for possible lags in adjustment); but it may be rising as well as falling (as Ricardo says) so long as it stays within those limits. Each point on that path is a short-run equilibrium; but at no point on it is the economy in a steady state until the final stationary state is reached.

When fixed capital is introduced there are greater difficulties. I much doubt if by Ricardo they were ever surmounted.

[11] As is done in the curve FF' in Figure 1.

needed for analysis of causation) but why they varied would not by the model be explained. But how, in a less ambitious model of this type, were wages and profits to be determined?

Ricardo already, they felt, had provided an answer. For the supply of land, in Ricardo, was already exogenous; and Ricardo had shown how the rent of land is determined. If labour and capital are applied in fixed proportions, their combination could be treated as a 'bundle'; the bundle would get its marginal product and the surplus would accrue as rent. This gave no solution for division between labour and capital; but was not the lack of a principle for that division, which from the viewpoint of a neo-classic marred the rent theory, due to the fixed proportion between capital and labour that was being assumed? As between them and land, the fixed proportion had already been abandoned; why not apply the same principle to labour and capital separately, and conclude that its own marginal product would accrue to each? All that was needed was an all-round abandonment of the fixed coefficients; factor prices (equilibrium factor prices) would then each be determined in the same way, by marginal productivity.[12]

The theory thus sketched has been savagely criticized; some of the criticisms are valid, but there are

---

[12] The marginal productivity theory, in this sense, already appears in Longfield (1834) and von Thunen (1850). Among the 'neo-classics' we find it in the early Marshall (see my review of Whitaker's *Early Economic Writings of Alfred Marshall* Econ. Jour. June 1976); but there are clear indications that Marshall later abandoned it. A later adherent was Pigou (*Economics of Welfare* 1920) on whose work the present writer's early work (*Theory of Wages* 1932) was largely based. It is not widely represented in the other 'neo-classics', Walras, Pareto or the Austrians. It has nothing to do with Marginal Utility (see p. 68 below).

some which are not. It cannot, if properly understood, be more than a static theory. Its field of application is to static causality: the comparison of actual performance, over what must be a fairly long period, when that is reduced to the static condition which most nearly corresponds to it, with the hypothetical static condition which would have existed if some data, in particular the supplies of the factors, had been different. That is a comparison which we may not want to make; but there are purposes, as has already appeared, for which it is quite sensible to make it. It is nevertheless apparent, when the issue is posed in this way, that it is quite hopeless to string such equilibria together, making them successive in time, so as to form a growth model. No means is shown, no means can be shown, by which an economy can pass from one such equilibrium to another. So nothing can be shown about the *accumulation* of capital.

Where the method belongs is in comparative statics; but even there it has weaknesses, which cannot be denied. First, it requires us to be able to say that when two static states are being compared, the volume of capital in the one *is* greater than in the other; it requires us, at least to that extent, to be able to measure capital. That is a formidable problem; though if we are resolute in insisting on the static comparison, and not constructing a growth model, it is perhaps not quite so formidable as has been sometimes supposed.[13]

A second weakness comes from the fact that the abandonment of the classical fixed coefficients is by no means pure gain. The fixed coefficients, as we saw, could be taken to be rather *firm*; the neo-classical

---

[13] I have discussed the measurement of capital on several occasions; the most recent, and most relevant, is in *Capital and Time*, ch. 13.

'Production Function' is by no means so firm. It is supposed to be the expression of a given 'technology', a set of techniques which *might be* employed, that actually employed being one of them. But *might be* in what sense? It may be granted that techniques do respond, sometimes at least, to changes in factor prices; but what usually happens is that a change in relative factor prices stimulates a search for a new technique which shall economize in that factor which has become relatively scarce. In the course of that search a new technique may well be discovered which it would have paid to adopt even though the factor-price change had not occurred. Such a technique, we are taught, should not be regarded as belonging to the old technology; its introduction would mark an *invention*. But is not the new technique, introduction of which would not occur without the factor-price change, but which was not known before the factor-price change, equally an invention? If we include such techniques in the original technology, are we not drawing its boundaries too wide? But if we exclude them, are we not drawing them too narrow? A Production Function, the technology of which includes no more than known techniques, leaves little scope for the adjustments which for marginal productivity are essential, even when that is taken in the strictest comparative statics sense. But if we include techniques that might be discovered, where do we draw a line?

A third weakness, which is of course notorious, concerns the apparent dependence of marginal productivity on a particular form of economic organization, commonly known as *perfect competition*. It is nowadays accepted that, at least since the Industrial Revolution, industry has never been perfectly competitive; though it may well have been justifiable for Ricardo to assume that in his time agriculture was perfectly competitive (and it should be noticed that

that was the only place where in his theory the
assumption was needed). Marshall had already recognized that industry cannot be perfectly competitive,
and that may well have been the reason which led him
to abandon, or at least to qualify, the marginal productivity theory, to which he had formerly adhered.[14] I am
nevertheless, for my own part, inclined to maintain
that the dependence of marginal productivity on perfect competition is not so complete as its critics would
suppose. I accept that from the point of view of the
firm, minimization of unit cost (of a given output)
cannot mean more than that the prices of *employed*
factors, in equilibrium will be proportional to their
marginal products; and if, as will happen in an imper-
fectly competitive industry, the firm is producing at
diminishing cost, this implies that the prices of these
factors will be (uniformly) less than the values of their
marginal products, since payment of all factors at their
full marginal products would swallow up more than is
available. But when the analysis is applied to a whole
economy, instead of a single firm, this should not be
driven too hard. It is true that the payment of all
factors at full marginal products implies that there are
constant returns to scale. Nevertheless, as we have
seen, we have a good deal of liberty about the kinds of
changes in technical coefficients which shall be admitted into an unchanged Production Function. So it is
not impossible (though it may be awkward) to classify
all changes in coefficients which are due to scale
economies as inventions; then (remembering, once
again, that we are making a static comparison, between states within which the scale of output is
unchanging over time) we may keep 'our' form of
Production Function free from scale economies, so
that the marginal products which are possible *within it*

---

[14] See note 12.

can still add up. I make no claim that this device is much to be recommended; but it is not excluded. Those economists (and they are not few) who still hold to marginal productivity, as an equilibrium condition of a static model, do have this way out.[15]

I have thought it worth while to give this amount of attention to these two static theories, the 'classical' steady state and the 'neo-classical' Production Function, since they are the main methods which have been developed by economists for the formation of a general, or 'macro', theory on static lines. Each has its adherents; the struggle between them, which began in the nineteenth century, has lately taken a new lease of life. The present writer, it should have been made evident, is not now an adherent of either. I am far too conscious of the weaknesses of each to be willing to commit myself to either; but I would not necessarily be unwilling to make use of the one, or the other, for some particular purpose, if a purpose is found for which its weaknesses do not matter too much.

It is easier, however, to recognize purposes, less 'general' purposes, for which we are happy to make do with something much simpler—with the *simple* version of the classical model which we found to be sufficient for the simple analysis which we took from Adam Smith. Thus it is that when dealing with international trade problems, we are often content to think of countries having 'resources' with greater or less 'productivity'; not distinguishing, that is, between the

---

[15] For further discussion of the device, which has been outlined in this paragraph, see pp. 331–350 in the *Commentary* which is annexed to the 1963 edition of my *Theory of Wages*. Those who are interested may also care to consult the paper 'Elasticity of Substitution again' which I published in *Oxford Economic Papers* November 1970. It is an improvement on some of the mathematics in the *Theory of Wages* Commentary.

separate, or separable, factors, of which these resources are composed. So we go back to something which is equivalent to a labour theory of value. We do not do so because we believe that costs are reducible to 'homogeneous labour'; only that it is sufficient, for particular purposes, to treat them as if they were expressible as quantities of homogeneous 'stuff'. This can be done (as was observed) if changes in the proportions in which factors are combined are not, for the problem in hand, of major importance; or when it is sufficient to suppose that prices are formed from labour costs by a constant 'mark-up'. And it is not only for static problems that we allow ourselves such simplifications; we also use them in the study of contemporaneous causation, as in the application of the Keynesian system. To that I shall be coming.

V
Contemporaneous causality—stocks and flows

The subject of this chapter, and also of the chapter on Keynesian analysis which follows it, is Contemporaneous Causality, a kind of causality which may have startled the reader when it was first proposed to him, but which I shall be maintaining to be the characteristic form of the causal relation in modern economics. That holds, not only for the Keynesian approach, but also for much work that is less ambitious—'micro' rather than 'macro'. I shall be showing that in economics it is likely to hold, as soon as time is taken seriously, as soon as we make a proper distinction between past and future.

In the static models, which we have been considering, time is not taken seriously; past and future are the same; they remain the same, as far forward, and as far back, as we care to look. That such constructions have some limited uses has not been denied; but there is so much of economic experience with which they cannot cope that we are bound to press on beyond them.

Much of the work of economists is concerned with the future, with forecasts and with planning. But forecasts are trivial and planning is useless unless they are based on fact; and the facts which are at our disposal are facts of the past. (It may be recent past, but it is past all the same.) The purpose of analysis, applied to those facts, is the explanation of what has happened—the explanation, that is, of economic history. Unless we have attempted such explanation, our forecasts can be no more than mere extrapolation; and we have learned, or should have learned, from statistical theory, how dubious extrapolation is. We have no reason to have confidence in it unless it is based on historical analysis; so, even if our business is with forecasts, of what is likely to happen, or with the probable results of policies to be adopted now, historical analysis comes first.

Now the facts of economic history belong, for the most part, to a particular kind of historical fact. We are accustomed, in general history—especially, perhaps, in political history—to think of facts as records of events, events which have occurred at particular dates, such as 1066, 1776, 1789, 1914 and so on; we know what these stand for. When history is told as a story, or as a drama, such dated facts are strung together. Economic history, by contrast, is rather barren of events. The facts of economic history are different.

There was indeed a stage, at the beginning of modern work on economic history, when it was customary to write it as if it were political history; pieces of legislation—the Corn Laws, the Poor Law and so on—being taken as typical events. But when questions were asked about the effects of those events, they could not be answered in those terms. What was then required was not records of events; what was wanted was statistics.

The economic historian, who is concerned with earlier ages, is still very short of statistics; though it is wonderful how much of them he has been able to piece together. For recent economic history they are plentiful; so it will be sufficient, for the present purpose, to confine attention to cases where there is no shortage. This perhaps is the point where the work of the economic historian, in the professional sense, diverges from the work of the applied economist. Our problems will be those of the applied economist.

Say then that he has his statistics, in the form of time-series, giving the values of some economic variables at particular dates in the past. These, it will be noticed, are not records of events; the dates are not selected because at them something unusual happened. A time-series is most useful when it is most continuous, with no political events, such as wars or revolutions, interrupting it. We can make most progress in interpreting it, or explaining it, when it goes on through interesting years, and dull years, together.

It must next be observed that there are two kinds of time-series, with different kinds of time-reference. In one of them each item relates to a point of time, in the other to a period. Perhaps one should say, with respect to the first, *is supposed to relate* to a point of time; for statistics take time to collect, so that the point of time which is intended cannot in practice be defined very narrowly. The distinction, however, is clear. We may take as an example, a leading example, of the first, a time-series which is derived from the population census; for what each census shows is the number of persons, and of various classes and groups of persons, who are found to be living in the country at a particular date. And as a leading example of the second, a time-series of production, which purports to show the values of goods produced in successive years, that is to say, during particular *periods*. All historical statistics are of one or other of these kinds, relating, an economist would say, either to stocks or flows.

The modern economist has learned much about the stock-flow distinction from the work of accountants; for it was the accountant, in carrying through the task that is laid upon him of giving a 'true and faithful' account of the performance of a business, who first found himself impelled to put his records into forms of each kind, which he sharply distinguished. He had, on the one hand, a stock account, the balance-sheet; and on the other a number of flow accounts (trading account, profit-and-loss account, and so on). The flow accounts showed what went on during the year; stock accounts what was at the beginning, and at the end. Already, in accounting, there were problems of fitting them together.

The modern economist has taken the hint and has learned to think in terms of *accounting periods*. An accounting period is not like the 'period' of statics, which goes on indefinitely; it is a historical period, with a beginning and an end. A whole economy, like a firm, will begin its accounting period with inheritance from the past of a given stock of equipment. Though new equipment may be added during the period, the beginning-stock sets limits upon production pos- sibilities; whatever is possible during the period must be consistent with it. The end-stock is not in the same way a limiting factor. It can be changed by current performance; it is nevertheless of great importance just how it is changed.

The fitting together of stocks and flows, as they appear in economics, is a good deal harder than in accounting; as we shall see, it is with no more than moderate success that it has been done. There are, however, some cases where it is unnecessary, or seems to be unnecessary; there is one of these which deserves some attention.

It occurs in the simplest form of demand study, the study from which econometrics began. If our statistic is a time-series of sales, sales to final consumers of a good which is non-durable, there must be negligible carry-over by consumers from one period to another;

so what happens within the period can be analysed without reference to beginning-stock and end-stock. The sale is a flow, extending over the period; so it is natural to look for causes which themselves extend over the period, which also are flows. Each period, then, can be treated separately; each is a separate 'experiment'. The fact that the periods are successive does not matter. If we have similar time-series for possible causes, we can proceed, by well-known statistical methods, to estimate the probable effect of each. If we allow ourselves to suppose that each cause enters linearly, we can fit a demand function of the form

$$y_t = a_1x_{1t} + a_2x_{2t} + \ldots + a_nx_{nt}$$

where y_t is the sale in period t, x_{1t}, ... x_{nt} are the values of the causes (as they were in period t) while the a's are constants which measure the 'power' of each cause.

Such a procedure (which, with mathematical variants, is very commonly practised) does nevertheless beg serious questions. In the first place, how do we know that y is effect, while the x's are causes? They are all of them flows extending over the period, so that there is no time-distinction between them, which (if it existed) might help. If we had taken one of the x's to be the effect, with y one of the causes, then (as is well known) we should have found a different relation. Secondly (even when that has been settled) how do we choose the x's that are to be included? We do have a means of rejecting a possible claimant; for if the best fit is found with $a_n = 0$ (so that we get the same fit whether or not x_n is included) then it is clear that x_n can be taken out. But it is not in practice possible to test for all variables that might conceivably be included; we must have some principle by which to decide in which directions we are to look. We must first decide on a list; then, from that list, some may be rejected.

These two decisions have to be made, the distinction of the effect and the list of possible causes, before the curve-fitting can start; in a practical case we may not bother about them, because we think them to be obvious. Yet they cannot be made without a theory. All causative analysis, as I have repeatedly emphasized, depends on theory. If we think the decisions to be obvious, that can only mean that we are taking the theory for granted.

It is my own view that the theory is not at all obvious; it needs quite careful statement if it is to be at all persuasive.[1]

We have already decided (when saying that there is to be no carry-over by consumers) that the causes are to operate through the behaviour of consumers; but if the amount acquired is to be a matter of consumers' behaviour, it must be implied that they are free to choose how much to acquire. (We are not, that is, dealing with a rationed market, whether the rationing is by a public authority or by the sellers.) If that is granted, it does follow that the amount purchased is the effect, while things which may influence the decision to buy will be causes.

We have to go that far; but it is usual to go further. It is assumed that consumers' decisions will be in accordance with what in the preceding chapter I called the Economic Principle—that when an opportunity for gain presents itself it will be taken. As that principle was used by the Classical Economists, such as Smith and Ricardo, it was confined in its application to the behaviour of producers; the innovation that was made

---

[1] Many of my readers will know that I have been over this ground before. The statement which I gave, nearly forty years ago, in *Value and Capital* (1939, ch. 1) is none too sure in its footing. That in my *Revision of Demand Theory* (1956, especially pp. 16–18) is much better; what I am saying here is I think consistent with it.

by the 'Marginal Utility Revolution' consisted in applying it to the behaviour of consumers also. The producer is earning money, so it is natural to take his gain to be expressed in money terms; but the consumer, as such, is spending money, not earning it, so the gain which he gets from his spending (from spending in one way rather than in another) is most naturally expressed in terms of something else, which is called 'utility'.[2] The consumer, who acts according to the Economic Principle, chooses his purchases so as to maximize utility.

If this assumption is to be useful for establishing causality (or any probability of causality) it must however be presumed that the utility function, which expresses utility as a function of quantities purchased, remains unchanged throughout the series of 'experiments'. That is to say, if in one year there is a gain in moving from one collection of quantities purchased to another collection, the same movement in another year must also register a gain. This, in relation to the econometric problem of analysing a time-series, is obviously a strong assumption, which we would not always want to make. So it is best[3] to regard the utility-maximizing principle as a means of classification, by which we can separate possible causes of changes in demand into two types: (1) those which lend themselves to interpretation as *economic* reactions to changes in his environment by a Representative Consumer, whose want-system, or utility function, remains invariable and (2) those which do not. Under the latter head would come such things as

---

[2] It is indeed possible, by the device of consumer's surplus, to find indirect ways of measuring utility gains in money terms; but these do not here concern us.

[3] As we saw at a corresponding point in the previous chapter.

changes in population, in the age-distribution of population, the degree of education and so on; these are
not excluded as possible causes, but we have to use our
judgement how far it is worth while to test them for
relevance.

It is only so far as the former are concerned that we
get help from formal theory. It indicates, at the least,
what are the economic variables, relating to the
period, which we have to consider: the price of the
commodity, the income of the consumers, and the
prices of the other things on which income might be
spent. Other influences than these having been
excluded by the use of the Economic Principle, these
are all that is left. Even so, if we had to take account of
all the other prices, of things on which income might
be spent, we should not be much further forward.
Some simplification, however, is possible. It may happen (as probably did happen at the time when the
marginal utility theory was first propounded) that the
money prices of many commodities are fairly stable.
Money could then be taken as a measure of purchas-
ing power over those commodities.[4] Income could be
measured in money; the price of the commodity,
demand for which is being analysed, could be
measured in money; and it would only be the prices of
those other commodities which were closely related to
the first commodity (as substitutes or complements to
it) that would have to be brought in explicitly. When
monetary stability of this sort is absent, we are
reduced to performing the analysis *in real terms*. That
is to say, we construct an artificial money, in terms of
which the prices of the background commodities can
(perhaps) be kept fairly stable; we measure income in
terms of the artificial money while the prices of the

---

[4] It is precisely in this sense that the term 'money' is used
in Marshall's demand theory.

foreground commodities (the commodity demand for which is being analysed, together with its complements and substitutes) are also reduced into terms of the artificial money. It must nevertheless be a question, in times of monetary disturbance, whether there is any method of 'deflating' into real terms which will give us the background stability which we require.

All this (and of course much more than this) can be said about the case of demand for a good which is non-durable; the case in which carry-over, at the beginning and end of the period, can be left out of account. In this case, but only in this case, can it be sufficient to consider, as possible economic causes, the flow variables which belong to the period: the income of the period, and the prices of the period (which also are flow variables, since they enter into flow accounts).[5] But even in the case of a good which itself is non-durable, it may not be sufficient, for related commodities may be of a different character. A leading example of this is the demand for motor spirit (petrol or gasoline). The stocks that are carried over by the consumer from one period to another may well be negligible; but the demand is highly complementary with demand for motor vehicles, stocks of which, most certainly, are carried over. The demand for petrol in the current period must be affected by the decisions that have been made to purchase cars in previous periods. But this does not mean that contemporaneous causality, in a demand study of this kind, has to be abandoned. It can be rescued (and in practice it clearly would be rescued) by replacing those previous decisions by the stock of cars, as it was at the beginning of the period, in which they are

---

[5] If prices were changing during the period, it is the average price which was ruling during the period which (presumably) must be taken.

embodied. This is an element in the opening stock of the accounting period; we must reckon it, as the accountant would do, to belong to the period. We need do no more than reckon the opening stock of cars as one of the causes of the demand for petrol during the period.

But surely (it will be objected) these are not contemporaneous; the beginning of the period must come before the period itself! The objection is natural, but it must be resisted. We can say, on the one hand, that the length of the period is arbitrary; if we were to shrink it to an 'infinitesimal length', the priority of the opening stock to the period which follows it would be negligible. But that, I think, is no more than an evasion. It is more to the point to insist that the stock of cars continues during the period (being added to, no doubt, by new production and subtracted from by scrapping) and that it is this stock, continuing during the period, which is properly to be reckoned as a cause of the demand for petrol during the period. The opening stock embodies the past decisions, but these are not the only decisions that affect the stock variable. The proper stock variable is a stock variable *of the period*, so it is contemporaneous.

It is true that if we turned our attention from the demand for petrol to the demand for the cars which are complementary with it we should have further complications. For there is then both a flow demand and a stock demand to be considered. This is at once apparent if we suppose that in some period the supply of new cars is interrupted; there would still be a market for cars, for the second-hand cars that are already in existence. There would thus be a stock demand, a demand which expressed itself at a point of time; but it would differ from the flow demands, which we have been considering hitherto, in another respect than its time-reference. The individual car-owner is still free, whether to retain the car that he owns or to sell it; but the whole body of car-owners (including potential car-owners) is not free to decide how many cars in total they will acquire, or retain; for the whole stock of cars, for the moment, is given. In this case, therefore, it is the price (or price-level) of the used cars which must be the effect, while the supply is a cause. And they are clearly contemporaneous.

When there is both a flow supply (of new cars) and a stock supply (of old cars carried over from the past) we would expect that the prices, in the two markets, would have to maintain some relation to each other. That is a problem which already arises, in the case of any particular durable good; but it also arises on a 'macro' scale, in relation to the capital stock of the whole economy. The first economist who appreciated this at all fully was Keynes. I shall say what I have to say about its appearance in his work in the following chapter.

VI
Contemporaneous causality in Keynes

I shall mean by the Keynes theory just the formal theory which has gone into the textbooks.[1] We have been forcibly reminded (by Leijonhufvud[2] and others) that there is much more in Keynes than there is in the formal theory; I fully agree. But what I need in this chapter, as an illustration of contemporaneous causality, is just the formal theory. It cannot, I think, be questioned that it is one of the things that are in Keynes. When we lose sight of him, he is further up the mountain; but this is a place where for a while he had pitched his tent. To have got so far as this was already an achievement; we do him honour, and no injustice, if we mark it by his name.

It is divided, as Keynes himself indicated, into three

---

[1] For the textbook formalization I must myself take some responsibility; for ISLM first saw the light in a paper of my own. ('Mr. Keynes and the Classics', *Econometrica* 1937; reprinted in my *Critical Essays*, 1967.) I have, however, continually repeated that I considered myself to be doing no more in that paper than arranging what then appeared to be a central part of Keynes's teaching, for expository purposes. I am sure that if I had not done it, and done it in that way, someone else would have done it very soon after.

[2] *On Keynesian Economics and the Economics of Keynes* (1968).

parts: (1) the consumption function, which relates income (Y) to investment (I); (2) the marginal efficiency of capital schedule, which relates investment to the rate of interest (r); (3) liquidity preference, which relates the rate of interest to the quantity of money (M). Since both I and Y are measured over a period, the first of these relations is clearly a flow relation; but the quantity of money is a stock, existing at a point of time, so the third is a stock relation. The status of the second is not so obvious. The *demand curve*, relating the demand for a commodity over a period to its price averaged over the period, may (as we saw) be taken to be a flow relation. The same might seem to hold for the relation between interest and investment; but here, as we shall see, there are complications.

I shall take the three relations in order, beginning accordingly with the consumption function and the Multiplier.

There are two versions of the Multiplier theory: the Kahn version, which is clearly sequential (so it does not belong in this chapter) and Keynes's version, which is not sequential (so it does). The Keynes version, as I can well remember from early discussions on the *General Theory*, is not at all easy to take. Modern students, indeed, have got used to swallowing it; but it may still be useful to set out, in the light of the distinctions that have been made in preceding chapters, just what is involved.

What is involved is a peculiar use of what I have called the *equilibrium method*. This can be seen most clearly if we take, as on former occasions, the historical application. We are seeking to explain the level of income (which, at a given level of money wages, carries with it the level of employment) that obtained in some particular past year, say 1975. We know the facts of that year, what investment (I) and income (Y) were in that year. We have to compare them with what they would have been if some *cause*, which in the present inquiry we are prepared to treat as exogenous, had been different. This is not on record; it can only be deduced with the aid of a theory. We have to construct a model, in which the exogenous element is allowed to vary, while other things, *so far as possible*, are to be kept unchanged.

Keynes was undoubtedly right in insisting that the model must be constructed consistently; so that the equality of saving and investment,[3] which is a pure accounting identity, must hold in the model, as it does in fact. And then, if there is a dependable relation between saving and income (according to which saving increases when income increases, but not to the same extent) an increase in income—from one state of the model to another—must be matched by an increase in saving, and so in investment. It will similarly hold, again just comparing states of the model, that an increase in investment must be matched by a more than equal increase in income (the Multiplier). If we prefer, as Keynes preferred (in this part of his theory) to treat investment as exogenous, it will be the second (Multiplier) form of the relation which we shall regard as important.

Just how far Keynes himself regarded his saving function (or consumption function) as dependable is, however, a question worth considering. We know that he was a sceptic about econometrics;[4] so he can hardly have fancied that it would be possible to calculate his function—the function to be applied to the analysis of some particular year ('1975')—by induction from the

---

[3] The familiar qualifications about imports and exports, taxation and government expenditure, may be left to the reader.

[4] The chief evidence for this is the Tinbergen review (see p. xii above).

behaviour of income and saving in previous years (back to 1965, or 1955). So he would not have expected it to be usable, in the manner which later became so fashionable, for projections, even for 'fine tuning'. I know myself, from my own recollections, that it was nearly a decade after my first acquaintance with the *General Theory*, before I realized that people were taking the function in that way.[5] It was not natural to take it that way when one first read the book.

It was natural to take the function as being theoretical; that is to say, as being based on reasoning, from rather obvious aspects of observed behaviour, as is commonly done in other parts of economics. This is a field where there is much scope for such reasoning. Extremely subtle work has been done, since Keynes's day, on 'optimal' or 'rational' saving; the beginning of that work, in the famous paper[6] by Keynes's own friend, Frank Ramsey, was certainly known to Keynes. Yet I would doubt how far he would have judged it to be relevant. It would have been sufficient, for his purposes, to think of the choice between saving and consumption as a simple choice between provision for the future and enjoyment in the present.[7] In

---

[5] If I had been working in London, during the War, I should no doubt have realized it sooner.

[6] 'A Mathematical Theory of Saving' (*Economic Journal* 1928).

[7] I have myself become convinced, after a good deal of work on the mathematical theory, that this simple way is in fact the right way of stating the issue. It is the assumption that planned expenditures, at different dates in the future, have independent utilities, which has been the foundation of most of the mathematical work; but this assumption I find quite unacceptable. As I said in *Capital and Growth* (1965, p. 261), 'If the successive consumptions have independent utilities, the amount of present consumption

reality (in '1975') some part of the income of the representative receiver was allotted to each ; and there would be no reason to suppose that the desire for either would be satiated. The two objectives are distinct; neither could possibly be an inferior substitute for the other; so the 'inferior goods' phenomenon is ruled out. Thus, if income were increased, there would be an opportunity for each to be satisfied better. The increment of income would be divided between them, which is what the Consumption Function says.

This, however, is rational behaviour; it is what we may reasonably expect (by analogy with what we know of the demand for commodities) the representative individual to plan to do, or to try to do. Whether he will succeed in doing what he plans to do is another matter. All we know about '1975' are the realized savings; we do not know what savings were planned to

---

which the chooser will be willing to give up, in order to be able to increase consumption in year 5 from so much to so much, will be independent of the consumptions that are planned for year 4 and year 6. It will be just the same, whether the increase in year 5 is to be a sudden spurt, out of line with its neighbours; or whether it is needed to fill a gap, to make up a deficiency which would otherwise have occurred in year 5, so raising the consumption of year 5 up to the common level. This is what is implied in the independence assumption; but when it is stated in those terms, surely it must be said that it cannot be accepted. The sacrifice which one would be willing to make to fill a gap must normally be much greater than what it be worth while to occur for a mere extra. ... It is nonsense to assume that successive consumptions are independent; the normal condition is that there is strong complementarity between them.'

If that is so, it is better to take provision for the future as a whole, treating it as a single 'commodity', than to bother ourselves about planned expenditures at *different* future dates.

be made. In the model, on the other hand, we do not have this information about realized savings; so all we can do is to say what we can, from theory, about planned savings, and then to assume that *in the model* planned savings and realized savings are the same. We must thus assume that the economy, in the model, is in equilibrium. That is why I say that the use of the Consumption Function to establish a Multiplier is an example of the equilibrium method.

It may perhaps be objected that equilibrium, in this statement, is being given a different sense than that which we have previously given to it.[8] I admit that there is a difference, but I think that there is continuity. We saw that in statics equilibrium could be defined as a condition in which all actors were taking all opportunities for gain that were open to them; and that the same concept could be taken over to the theory of consumer demand, where it would mean that each consumer was maximizing his *utility*. Saving is an activity which has a time-dimension, which in those other applications was neglected or suppressed. Here it cannot be neglected; so ignorance of the future, at the time when a decision is taken, is a pregnant cause of failure to reach a utility optimum. It is a natural extension of the equilibrium concept to say that there is equilibrium, in respect of saving, when such failure is absent.

It must be insisted that equilibrium, in any of these senses, is a characteristic of a model. But if the fundamental meaning is that opportunities that are open are being taken, how can equilibrium be consistent with unemployment (as Keynes said it is)? What about the unemployed? Could they not find opportunities opened to them by under-cutting the employed, offering to work at lower wages? To this, as is well known,

---

[8] See above, pp. 45–6 and 67.

there are several answers;[9] perhaps the simplest is the best. There is no reason, in a model, why we should not take the level of money wages to be exogenous—to be determined by conditions which the model does not seek to explain. A model which is restricted by this condition can be in equilibrium, so far as *other* choices are concerned, even though there is unemployment.[10]

There is one further point about the Multiplier that needs a mention, since it is very important in relation to policy, though in the historical application it does not arise. In the historical application, we start off knowing what I and Y were in the year that is under study. So we can just ask: if I had been different, what would have been the effect on Y? But in the policy case, we start with some measure that is to be taken

---

[9] They are set out in my *Crisis in Keynesian Economics*, in the chapter on Wages.

[10] I doubt if there is any concept of equilibrium usable in economics which is truly 'general', in the sense that there are no choices which might conceivably be open to the actors but which have not been, for the purpose of the model, deliberately closed. The Walrasian equilibrium itself, which is commonly regarded as a pattern of general equilibrium, is not general in this unrestricted sense. The perfect competition assumption under which it operates deliberately excludes coalitions between the parties, such as in practice, if they were not prevented by regulation, would surely enable some of them to gain a monopoly profit. But there is nothing sacred about this particular restriction; though we may have got used to it, and find it hard to replace it by another. In Marshall's economics the relativity of equilibrium ('particular equilibrium') is throughout implied. Keynes, having been brought up as a Marshallian, would naturally have thought in terms of this relativity, even though he was concerning himself with the equilibrium of a whole economy, rather than with that of a particular industry.

(say) to increase investment; but we do not know what
will be the actual increase in investment, above what
would otherwise have obtained, which will result.
Even if we can put a figure on the primary increase in
investment, that does not tell us what secondary
effects on other elements in investment it will have, or
is likely to have. Some of these (running-down of
stocks) may be in the direction of offsetting the
primary increase; but there are others which may go
the other way.[11] It is the resultant increase in investment, after these secondary effects have been allowed
for, to which the Multiplier has to be applied.

I proceed to the second of Keynes's relations, the
marginal efficiency of capital, investment as a function
of interest. There is here no question that, in Keynes's
intention, interest is the cause and investment the
effect. The name he gave to his function was nevertheless unfortunate, for it invited confusion with the *marginal productivity of capital*, a static concept which was
familiar to his readers; that static concept is not naturally, or at least necessarily, read the same way. And
Keynes's concept is very different from the static concept; it is forward-looking, ignorance of the future
being essential to it.

There can of course be no question that Keynes's
insistence on the forward-looking character of his
investment function is important and valuable. But it
does have some puzzling features. One may indeed
ask whether in a theory which is to be used for the
study of causal relations, along with the (contemporaneous) multiplier, it can properly find a place.

It is true that at first sight there seems to be no
difficulty. Take, once again, the historical application.
We know what investment was in the year '1975'; we

_____

[11] I have discussed these secondary effects, at some length,
in the chapter on the Multiplier in *Crisis*, just cited.

are inquiring why it was not higher (or lower). The causes to which Keynes would direct our attention seem straightforward; even a pre-Keynesian economist, confronted with the historical problem, would have argued in much the same way. Investment would have been higher if technical progress had thrown up better opportunities for investment (even a static theory would have to have found some way of taking account of that). It would also have been higher if business had been more optimistic, or more confident; that is much emphasized by Keynes, but 'waves of optimism and pessimism' were not unknown to his predecessors. And it might also have been higher if it had been easier for businesses to raise capital—this last being symbolized by Keynes in the form of saying that the rate of interest had been reduced.

All of these causes could be treated by the historian as being contemporaneous, like the Multiplier—relating to the same year '1975' and continuing over that period.

It is when we look at the matter more closely that the difficulties appear. Optimism, and confidence, are states of expectation: expectation that things affecting choice, but over which the chooser has no control, will turn out favourably, or will not turn out very unfavourably. At the moment of choice, these things are in the future. It is the fact that they belong to the future that gives them their peculiar quality. Over a period, however, the future moves. At the beginning of January of the year, the whole year is in the future; the future consists of that year and of what may lie beyond it. In July, no more than half of the current year is in the future; so the content of what is in the future has changed.

And there is more than that which must have changed. Future events, the future events that are expected, have a double time-reference; they have a date in calendar time, and they also have a date with respect to the present. August, say, is a month of holidays; it is known that there will be holidays in August; but in January August is six months away, in April it is no more than three months away; so on the second way of reckoning its date has changed. It follows that it is quite difficult to give a meaning to the statement that expectations are the same in April as in January—as, if the 'marginal efficiency of capital' is to remain unchanged from January to April, we should apparently require them to be.

For his own purposes, Keynes cut this knot. He confined attention to Fixed Capital Investment, the incentive to which, as he insisted, depended on expectations; but the expectations were (mainly) of the further future, of what was to happen *after* the end of the year. Though the distance of that, from the present, would change as the year proceeded, it (or most of it) would be so far in the future that the change in its distance would not much matter. So to this extent one could talk, and think, of unchanged expectations over the period.

That is all very well; there are purposes (I am prepared to believe) for which it is good enough. But for a full understanding of what is involved, it may be wise to be more critical, or more pedantic. If we refuse to accept Keynes's line of escape, what can we do?

The only alternative is to have recourse, as before, to the Equilibrium Method. One can construct a model in which expectations can be described as remaining unchanged, over a period, provided that *within the period* expectations are correct. What was expected in January to happen in June does happen in June; what was expected to happen in September does happen in September. So expectations, which relate to the future, pass smoothly into experience of the past, without the figures that are set upon them having to be changed. Thus we can, in equilibrium (but only in equilibrium) speak of unchanged expectations, over the period; though admitting that during the period some of these expectations will have turned into realities.

As for the expectations of the further future, which, even at the end of the year, remain expectations, it is easier to say that nothing is to have happened within the year which changes them. So nothing is to have happened within the year which has been unexpected.

A model of this kind is not realistic; it makes no claim to be realistic. We are just to use it as a standard of comparison with the actual. For the historical application, at least, it is not inappropriate. We admit that in actuality, in '1975', things that were unexpected did happen, so that there was no such equilibrium during that year. But the model is to show us what *would have happened* if some cause had been different. It would seem fair to say that since it is our model, our construction, it should not admit of unexpected events, since from our point of view nothing in the past can be unexpected. So the model can be, indeed should be, in equilibrium; though reality is not.

But how will this work with the third part of the Keynes theory, the liquidity preference relation, between the rate of interest and the supply of money? This, as we saw, and as Keynes repeatedly emphasized, is a stock relation, or balance-sheet relation, which refers to a point of time, not to a period. How is it to be fitted in with the other relations, when they are taken to refer to the period? This is the same question, it may be noted in passing, as arose in the old-fashioned quantity theory; there, it was long ago recognized, we have to introduce velocity to serve as a bridge. Where is the 'velocity bridge' in the Keynes theory? It seems to be missing.

It will not do to fall back on sequence: to say that

what is represented by M and by r is the liquidity position at the beginning of January, the cause from which I and Y, during the year, follow as effects. For the effect of Y on desired holdings of money, which certainly is a part of the Keynes construction, is one that goes on during the year. I can see no way out except to suppose that the balance-sheet relation is itself a relation that goes on during the year—perhaps in terms of an average of balance-sheets over the year. If that can be done, everything becomes annual, and the way is open for an interpretation of the whole Keynes construction, all three parts of it, in terms of Contemporaneous Causality.

But can it be done? Must we not, in attempting to do it, encounter the former objection, our expectations paradox, in a form that makes it harder to avoid it? How can we construct a demand for money schedule which is to remain valid over a period, under suitable condition of 'other things being equal'? That such a schedule may be postulated at a point of time may perhaps be granted; it is the summing it, or averaging it, or compounding it, over the period, that is the trouble. It is obvious, indeed only too obvious, that the same balance-sheet with just the same assets and liabilities may appear, with expectations as they were on the first of January, to be quite liquid; but with expectations as they are on the first of April, it may not be liquid at all. And how can expectations in January, and expectations in April, be the same?

For it is not at all easy, in this case, to fall back on the Equilibrium method. We cannot escape by saying that if things turn out as expected, then expectations (which have turned into experiences) are unchanged. For an essential characteristic of liquidity is that it is a matter of *uncertain* expectations. The expectations relating to April that could be formed in January were uncertain expectations; but when April is past, the experiences relating to April, which have replaced them, are certain. Thus we cannot avoid the transition in the present from uncertainty to certainty; past and future are inherently different, and cannot be 'averaged'. For this reason alone we seem driven to the conclusion that the Equilibrium method, applied to liquidity over a period, will not do.

There is, however, a possible way (a perhaps no more than just possible way) of saving it. We must evidently refrain from supposing that the expectations, as they were before April, of what is to happen after April were precise expectations, single-valued expectations; for in a model with single-valued expectations there can be no question of liquidity. And we must also refrain from the conventional representation of uncertain expectations in terms of mean and variance, since that makes them different in kind from the experiences that are to replace them. There is, however, a third alternative. Suppose we make them expectations that the values that are expected, of the variables affecting decisions, will fall within a particular range. That leaves room for liquidity, since there are no certain expectations of what is going to happen; but it also makes it possible for there to be an equilibrium, in the sense that what happens falls within the expected range. A state of equilibrium is a state in which there are no surprises. What happens (during the period) falls sufficiently within the range of what is expected for no correction of expectations to be necessary. If the Equilibrium method is to be carried through in all parts of the Keynesian construction, something like this would appear to be required.

Even so, it appears that the weakest part of the Keynesian model, the conventional Keynesian model, is after all the Liquidity Preference relation, which from other points of view, perhaps more important points of view, is its characteristic feature. Liquidity, it turns out, is not at home with Equilibrium; and is therefore not at home with Contemporaneous Causality. We shall find a better place for it in the chapter that follows.

VII
Sequential Causality—Lags and Reserves

I come at last to sequential causality, in which effect follows cause. This is the plain man's idea of causality, so it was the natural, indeed the inevitable, kind of causality with which to begin; the others, which in abstract are less familiar, had to be built up from it. But it is also the natural kind with which to end, for in concrete cases it is often the most difficult. In economics, as we shall see, it can be formidable.

It always involves an additional complication. For if we are to assert that A was a cause of B, the time at which B is dated being later than the time of A, do we not need something more than the logical connection so far considered? Do we not require an answer, or something in the way of an answer, to some supplementary questions? First, what is to be supposed to have happened between the two dates? Secondly, why did just so much time elapse between them, neither more nor less? It is evident that these are related questions; an answer to the first will help us to answer the second. But unless we can provide some acceptable answer to these supplementary questions, our statement of causality, of sequential causality, is not well established.

In narrative history, in political, military or diplomatic history, the supplementary questions are familiar. We are quite accustomed, in that context, to think of the causal connection as belonging to a process—a causal chain. A was a cause of A_1, A_1 of A_2 and so on; then A_n was a cause of B. At each of these steps there is the same logical connection. Though it will often be the case that there is no direct evidence for the intervening stages, the historian is satisfied if he can reconstruct them, in a way which is not inconsistent with such evidence as he possesses. He is content, that is, if he can tell an intelligible story.

Up to a point, it is much the same in economics. But the causal chains with which the economist is concerned have, at least for the most part, a rather special character. Economics, as I began by observing,[1] is concerned with decisions; decisions come in as the intermediate stage in most of its causal processes. The immediate cause of an economic effect is, nearly always, a decision by someone; or it may be the combination of decisions that were made by different people. But it is not enough, in economic analysis, to refer the effect to the decision; we are also concerned with the reasons for the decision, the causes of the decision. Thus even the simplest case of sequential causation in economics has two steps in it: a prior step, from the objective cause to the decisions that are based on it, or influenced by it, and a posterior step, from the decisions to their (objective) effects. With respect to the decision, the prior step is one of formation, the posterior of execution. Each of these steps may take time, so the total *lag* between cause and effect consists of two parts, prior and posterior. In order to explain the lag, which the posing of the supplementary questions impels us to try to do, we have to explain the prior lag *and* the posterior lag.

---

[1] See above, pp. 5–11. The whole of that concluding section of Chapter I is relevant to this chapter.

These, it can readily be seen, raise quite different problems.

Like the historian, the economist will often be concerned with chains of causation; but each link in his chain will, in general, consist of these two steps. In each link of the chain decisions will be intermediate.

Let me give some examples. I shall take them, as will clearly be convenient, from the Keynesian field we have lately been discussing. Take first the Consumption Function, now to be sequentially considered. An increase in income, or in spending power, is here the objective cause; the increase in consumption is the effect; decisions to increase consumption are intermediate. So long as the consumption is consumption of non-durable goods, of which there are plenty in the shops, the posterior lag may be negligible; but the prior lag is not necessarily negligible. Consumption over time is inter-related; so the impact of an increase in income, which may be regarded at first as temporary, does not necessarily show itself all at once. If the consumption takes the form of expenditure on durables, such as housing, the posterior lag may be long—for example, if the decision is to order the building of a house, building which takes much time. And there is much reason, in this latter case, why the prior lag also should be considerable.

Take next the case of the effect of costs on prices—the famous 'cost-push'. If the manufacturer is not bound by long-term contracts, he can raise the prices of his products just when he decides to do so; so, once again, there is no posterior lag. The prior lag, on the other hand, must in this case be of great importance, for it can be very variable. He has to find out how far he can safely raise prices, by observing the behaviour of his competitors (domestic and foreign), and by considering the probable course of public policy on level of demand and on protection (by exchange depreciation or otherwise) against foreign competition. It cannot be assumed that he will quickly raise prices in correspondence with costs, though there are occasions when he is likely to do so.

The first of these examples is an effect on quantities, the second on prices; in most economic causations the effect is on one or the other.[2] Whichever it is, the posterior lag is fairly straightforward. It may be long, as when the decision is to start a new productive process; but even so it is fairly dependable. Not, of course, completely dependable; the process may be disrupted by labour troubles, or by shortages of materials that are required in its later stages. The ways in which completion may be delayed by the scarcities that develop at the top of a boom are notorious. Still, important as these things are, to the economist they are fairly manageable.

The prior lag is much more tricky. For the objective cause does not necessarily compel a reaction; it is (as has often been said) a 'signal', and the reaction to the signal may be fast or slow. Economists did at one time work with models in which there were many signals that were imperative; and it may be that there was a time when that was not unrealistic.[3] If the worker is dependent upon wages paid weekly, has no borrowing power and little past savings, a fall in his wages must reduce his expenditure; while if the capitalist is faithful to the precept of living within his income,[4] the same

---

[2] Employment, of course, is a quantity.

[3] So it was that economists got into the habit of talking about the 'price-mechanism'. But it is only when signals are imperative that their action is mechanical.

[4] It will be noticed that it is implied in this example that the prior reaction may be different, not only because of different interpretations, by the agent, of the objective cause, but also because of characteristics, inherited or acquired, of the agent himself. These, as was shown in a previous

reduction in his expenditure must generally follow when there is a fall in the dividends, or rents, that he receives. But even in these cases the signal is less imperative when it goes the other way. Neither the worker nor the capitalist is obliged to spend more when his income rises.

The absence of reserves, either in the form of liquid assets or of assured borrowing power, is a severe constraint on freedom; it must therefore be expected that the decision-maker will seek to remove it, if that can be done at reasonable sacrifice, so far as he can. So the characteristic form of a modern economy is one in which many of those who make decisions have some reserves. They are accordingly not bound to respond to the signals; even if the signal persists, they have time to react. So the signal is less imperative, and therefore less dependable.

It is not at all necessary that the reserves take a financial form, though they often do so. The same delay may occur through the possession of unsold stocks. Take the simple case in which the objective cause is the expansion of demand for a particular product, an expansion which is expressed, objectively, by an increase in sales. If there are no stocks, there cannot be an increase in sales; all that can happen is an increase in orders. But if there are stocks, the initial increase in sales must show itself in a depletion of stocks; the seller, however, is at liberty to decide whether the depletion is tolerable, or whether it must be made good without delay. That is a matter of his

---

passage (p. 44 above) are usually relegated by economists to the status of 'obstacles'; but that is no reason for denying their importance, nor for refusing to submit them to analysis. I think of course chiefly of the work of Weber and Tawney, on religion and the rise of capitalism; but less 'sociological' matters such as the development of an ability to calculate fall, in principle, into the same category.

interpretation of the signal; so the impact effect of demand upon supply is a matter of interpretation. If the increased demand continues, there must sooner or later be an effect on production; that is easy, but how long it takes for the effect to materialize is quite a tricky matter.[5]

The same thing happens, in reverse, with a fall in demand; stocks may be allowed to pile up, until they become intolerable. But it is not the stocks themselves that become intolerable (though there may be a problem of storage); it is the financial effect of accumulating them that is the crux. More and more of the seller's capital becomes locked up in the unsold stocks, so his financial reserves continually fall. Even if he borrows to finance his holdings, his liquidity deteriorates.

The larger are the firm's financial resources, the longer it can resist; but it does not have to hold out until they are exhausted. If it is at once apparent that the reduction in demand is likely to be permanent, steps to reduce supply can be taken at once. The reserves confer the ability to delay reaction, but do not oblige it.

When we turn to consider a different type of reaction, reaction to an objective change which provides a new opportunity, there is a further distinction to be made. We must distinguish between the perception of

---

[5] I have myself constructed a couple of (rather mathematical) models designed to show the ways in which delayed reaction on production to a change in demand may set up 'inventory cycles'. These had to be constructed on the assumption that the reaction followed some simple rule; and (as I showed) the substitution of one rule for another (either being fairly plausible) makes a significant difference. I came to the conclusion that 'we are unable to simulate the behaviour of intelligent business management by any simple rule' (*Capital and Growth*, 1965, p. 102). That is the same thing as I am saying here.

the opportunity (the date at which the desire to make the decision first appears) and the possibly much later date at which action is taken upon it. If we take the latter to be the date of the decision, in the sense of the preceding discussion (as I think we should) then the prior step itself must be divided into two parts: the first proceeding from the objective cause to the perception of the opportunity which it offers—this being essentially a matter of information—while the second, a matter of negotiation, being that in which arrangements for making the decision effective are made. These in their turn may be of several kinds.

The most obvious is the need for capital to begin the new process. Here again we see the advantage that comes from the possession of liquid reserves, which if they are sufficient for the requirement (it is of course rare that they will be sufficient for a large requirement) can enable the stage of negotiation to be dispensed with, so far as the raising of capital is concerned. So here they shorten the delay of the negotiation stage. And even if they are not wholly sufficient for the requirement, some contribution from the firm's own capital may be expected to make it easier, and quicker, to raise the rest, since the risk that remains to be borne by those who supply the rest is reduced.

But it is not only in terms of the raising of capital that negotiation may interpose a delay. Land may have to be acquired; and that, notoriously, can be a lengthy process. Specialized labour also may have to be acquired (as for instance suitable managers); that can take time too. There are all these causes of delay even in the 'free' economy. They are replaced, in socialized and semi-socialized economies, by the need to get permissions and licences; but these, in practice, are also time-consuming.

I return to the question of liquidity. Putting the

cases we have been considering together, it will be seen that the possession of liquid funds always favours expansion. More precisely, it facilitates expansion (reckoning resistance to contraction as relative expansion); it does not oblige expansion, but always facilitates it. That is the general rule about liquidity; the way in which liquidity appears in the formal Keynes theory, as a relation between the 'supply of money' and the 'rate of interest' is no more than a special case. That is the way in which liquidity appears on financial markets; but the general concept of liquidity is much wider.

We should look, in every case, not only in the financial case, at the balance-sheet of the operator or decision-maker. The liabilities of any concern are financial; but it is characteristic of the financial firm (whether it be a bank, or investment trust, or pension fund, or stock exchange operator) that its assets (or at least that part of its assets with which it does its business) are financial also. It is characteristic of the non-financial firm that most of its assets are *real*, not financial; though it will usually have some financial assets, as well as financial liabilities. The liquidity problem of the financial firm is a question of the relative liquidity of its financial assets; it is operating upon a 'spectrum' of such assets, in the manner that has been analysed by Keynes (and others). The liquidity problem of the non-financial firm is a matter of the relation between its real assets, on the one hand, and its financial assets (and liabilities) on the other. Each, however, is fundamentally the same kind of problem.

For the meaning of liquidity is the same in each case. Liquidity is freedom. When a firm takes action that diminishes its liquidity, it diminishes its freedom; for it exposes itself to the risk that it will have diminished, or retarded, its ability to respond to future opportunities. This applies both within the financial sphere and outside it. I have myself become convinced that it is outside the financial sphere (very inadequately considered, in relation to liquidity, by Keynes) that liquidity is potentially of the greater importance.

This is because the decisions that affect the liquidity of the non-financial firm are larger relative to its business than those that affect the liquidity of the financial firm. In the case of the financial firm, the acquisition, for money, of a security of uncertain value makes it less liquid; this is because of the risk that at the moment when the money is wanted for some other purpose, the value of the security will be *abnormally* low, so that the opportunity cost of taking the other opportunity will be abnormally high. The financial firm, however, in the course of its ordinary business, is continually acting in such a way as to diminish or to increase its liquidity by small amounts. Liquidity preference, for the financial firm, is a matter of marginal adjustments, as Keynes very rightly saw. But the liquidity problem of the non-financial firm is not, as a rule, a matter of marginal adjustments.

It is true that the changes in its position that occur in the course of its ordinary business do produce marginal changes in its liquidity; there will, for instance, be seasonal peaks in its out-payments, but these are not usually of major importance. Such changes in liquidity do not as a rule affect policy, though they will if they build up, as we saw in the case of unsold stocks. But the most important cases in which liquidity becomes a serious issue are those when opportunities arise for an increase in investment, outside the ordinary day-to-day running of the business. For such investment is very likely to affect the liquidity of the firm in a notable manner. If it finances the investment from its own resources, its holding of financial reserves is directly diminished; if it finances it by borrowing, it uses up some part of the credit line it can call on. In either case, the danger of finding itself in an illiquid position is brought nearer. And illiquidity, to the industrial firm, is not just a matter of making itself unable to take advantage of some marginal opportunity; it is a danger of losing some degree of independence, by putting itself to some degree under the control of those who have lent to it. There are many ways in which that can occur, as we know from much experience, well short of bankruptcy; it is a great mistake to think of the liquidity of the producer purely in terms of profit and loss.

It is here, I think, that Keynes went most seriously wrong. It was very wrong to think that investment is governed by the rate of interest, as if any concern that wanted to invest could always raise as much capital as it required at a ruling interest rate. Rates of interest, at the most, are an index of liquidity; they are not by any means always a perfect index.

There is much to be said for beginning the study of liquidity, in economic theory, by considering a model in which, as a first step, neither interest rates nor any other prices change.[6] It might as well, again as a first step, be a closed economy. It could then be divided into three sectors: (1) Monetary Authority—Central Bank and Government (2) Financial Sector—banks and other financial institutions (3) the rest of the economy, which may be called 'Industry'. The Monetary Authority in a closed economy has no liquidity problem, though it may have a problem of watching over inflation, which has somewhat similar characteristics. (In an open economy it has that, and a problem of international liquidity as well.) Each of the concerns in the other two sectors has its own liquidity

---

[6] I have tried to construct such a model on pp. 75–9 of my *Economic Perspective* (1977). In what I am saying here I am following that discussion fairly closely.

problem; and since there will be much lending and borrowing within the sectors, the liquidity of the firms within the sectors is not adequately described by considering the liquidity of the sector as a whole. Nevertheless, in a model which should claim to be no more than the foundation of a theory, it may be sufficient to look at the relations between the sectors, neglecting the relations between the firms that compose them.

We would thus confine attention to the consolidated balance-sheets of the sectors. In these money appears as a liability of the Monetary Authority sector, and as an asset for the Financial Sector and for Industry. In the case of the Financial Sector it appears as a liquid asset, but most of the money that is held by Industry will be employed in circulating Industry's inputs and outputs, so the main liquid asset of Industry may be taken to consist of interest-bearing securities. (It is indeed true that in very static conditions, when prices are stable and interest rates very low, it may not much matter to industry whether it holds its reserves in the form of securities or in money form; but when interest rates are high, and especially in times of inflation when there is a *real* loss from holding money balances, it is reasonable to suppose that the reserves of industry will be mostly held in the form of securities, which—on consolidation—must either be liabilities of the Monetary Authority or of the Financial Sector. This is not inconsistent with the holding of money by the Financial Sector as a liquid asset; for, as we saw, the purposes for which the one sector and the other require a liquid asset are different.)

Now let us suppose that Industry seeks to expand production, whether it is production of capital goods or consumption goods does not matter. Inputs come before outputs, so the first requirement is for additional money to pay for the inputs; and if the higher level of production is to be maintained, the money will need to be kept within the industrial sector, to circulate the increased output. Where is this money to come from? It could come directly from the Monetary Authority—that is to say, in a practical case, from the Government; though the money advanced will be matched by a debt, from Industry to Government, that debt may well be in such a form as not to diminish the liquidity of Industry. Thus expansion of industry, which is matched by an increase in money supply, creates, as a rule, no problem of liquidity. But suppose that it is not so matched; suppose that the balance-sheet of the Monetary Authority remains unchanged. The additional money must then be drawn from the Financial Sector (unless industry has some reserves which, contrary to what has been said, are held in monetary form). But though the money must be drawn from the Financial Sector, this may be done in either of two ways.

On the one hand, money may be borrowed from the Financial Sector. The Financial Sector then acquires Industrial securities, liabilities of Industry, in place of money; so its liquidity, in terms of its consolidated balance-sheet, is directly reduced; it has just acquired a less liquid asset in place of one that was more liquid. Alternatively, if Industry finances the expansion by exchanging some of its own reserves (of financial securities) for money, the Financial Sector gives up liquid assets against a reduction in its own liabilities; though the reduction in its money holding is a loss in liquidity, the reduction in its liabilities is something to set on the other side. So the difference between the two methods appears to be a question of the distribution of the loss in liquidity between the Sectors. On the one route the loss falls mainly on the Financial Sector; on the other a more considerable part is left to be borne by the Industrial.

But there is more to the difference than that. For

when it is possible for Industry to finance the expansion from its own resources, even if these are reserves of financial securities (which could not serve as reserves unless they were readily marketable), the initiative in the financing remains with Industry; it does not have to ask the consent of financiers, as it must do on the other route. So the stage of negotiation, which we previously detected as an element in the causal chain, when that was considered sequentially, must therefore be shorter (so far at least as the capital requirement is concerned) when Industry can expand by use of its resources. One must not press the point too hard, since re-distribution of funds within the industrial sector (which may well be required, even if the sector as a whole has ample reserves) will also require negotiation. It is nevertheless not hard to find cases, important cases, when the distinction is important.

For consider the application to a single country, which is not a closed economy. Its Monetary Authority will then have problems of liquidity which, even with flexible exchanges, cannot be overlooked. The alleviation of strain by extension of the money supply is accordingly no longer a simple matter. One can see that in this case the possession of liquid funds by Industry will make it easier for opportunities to be taken quickly than if such reserves were absent or scarce. But successful expansion by Industry is very likely to put such resources into the hands of the successful firms; their position is strengthened not only because they have profits to invest, but also because they can seize the opportunities that are presented to them quickly. We know that successful development makes for a strong economy, in which 'stop-go' pressures on liquidity are infrequent. The present analysis suggests that the effect goes both ways. Successful growth makes for conditions in which liquidity constraints are of little consequence; but these, in their turn, are conducive to growth. In the weak economy, there are the same connections—in reverse. Economics is full of such 'virtuous' and 'vicious' circles: 'to him that hath shall be given'. It must nevertheless be insisted, in accordance with the principles laid down at the beginning of this essay,[7] that while such theories (this is a theory) are indispensable for the understanding of the past, they need not be taken to be binding for the future. From every weakness there is a way out, if it can be found.

I make no pretence that what has been said in the preceding pages is anything more than the beginning of a theory of liquidity. Even on the most abstract level, there is much that remains to be done. And before the theory could be applied, it would need to be interpreted in terms of institutional settings, which vary from country to country, and within each country from one time to another. At that stage it could of course pick up a good deal that has been done, especially by monetary economists, in relation to particular problems. But most of that lies in the future.

My purpose in going so far in that direction as I have just been doing has been different. My ultimate concern, in this chapter and in the three which have preceded it, has been to show that the squabbles of theorists—'classics' 'neo-classics' 'Keynesians' 'post-Keynesians' 'monetarists' even 'neo-Marxists'— which have become so arid when they are confined to theory, do, in the light of application, take on a different colour. The application I have been concerned with is not application to policy—that is indeed an important matter, which of course deserves attention, but I am not giving it attention here. The application with which I have been concerned is explanation; when we

---

[7] P. 11 above.

seek to identify a cause we seek to explain. I have tried to show that there are different kinds of causality in economics; and that to each kind there is, or can be, a kind of theory that corresponds.

To static causality corresponds static theory: the part of economic theory that is most completely developed, but which leaves even those most devoted to it unsatisfied, since its field of application is so narrow. The questions to which it can be applied cannot be urgent. To contemporaneous causality corresponds the (formal) theory of Keynes, and in 'micro' contexts that of Marshall, a theory which by now is also well-developed (and which even now would be better understood if it were not so often confused with static theory). A considerable part of the practical problems of contemporaneous causation that arise in our experience can be dealt with fairly well by this corresponding theory. I said, when I began my discussion of contemporaneous causality,[8] that it is the 'characteristic form of the causal relation in modern economics'. That may have startled the reader when it was first presented to him; I would nevertheless hold to it. It is because of its ability to deal, up to a point, with these problems that Keynesian economics has had its success.

It is nevertheless not surprising that economists, even the most 'Keynesian' ones, have become dissatisfied with it; for there are so many questions to which we desire to have answers with which it cannot cope. But they do little more than register their discontent when they search the scriptures, looking, in particular, for the abundant hints in Keynes's work that he himself was looking beyond the formal theory. I have been trying to show that the further development of theory, which I agree is required, should begin with an

[8] Above, p. 61.

attempt to identify the questions it will have to be concerned with. These, I have tried to show, are in essence questions of sequential causality. We have so far no more than the beginning of a theory which will help us with such questions; but we do have a beginning. The challenge I am presenting to economists is to go on from it.

What I have said in this chapter may also be summed up in another way. May it not be that the remarkable differences between the growth rates of productivity, in countries which have (apparently) access to the same improvements in technology, are to be ascribed, in part, perhaps even in main part, to differences in the *speed* in which they can respond to new opportunities? We have seen several reasons why there may be such differences. The liquidity point, which I have just been making, is one of them; the firm that can innovate from its own financial resources does not have to waste time in negotiating with bankers and other suppliers of credit. But more important in practice, in some cases that are easy to name, is the time that is spent in negotiating with trade unions and with government departments. But it does not follow, on this line of thought, that maximum speed will be achieved in the text-book 'laisser-faire' economy, a multitude of small firms that are left to themselves. For the time of transmission of an improvement from one of these firms to others may again be considerable. So perhaps the best way to have a high growth rate is to have large firms that are big enough to have the government, and (somehow) the unions, in their pockets! Not an agreeable solution! Most people would think it worthwhile to sacrifice something in growth rate to avoid it.

VIII
Probability and Judgement

When the Manchester Statistical Society (one of the earliest of such societies[1]) was founded in 1833, statistics meant social and economic statistics; and that was the meaning that was generally given to the word for many decades after that date. But as time went on, much the same methods as were first associated with the analysis of that material proved to be usable for other material; and (I think one may now say) better adaptable to other material. Thus modern statistical theory, which has developed into a formidable branch of mathematics, finds its most important applications in the natural sciences—as in some branches of physics, 'statistical mechanics', and in biology. It has practical uses in industry, but chiefly in those (very common) cases in which industrial production has become scientific—so that the production of each unit of product partakes, to some extent, of the nature of an 'experiment'. It also has uses in agricultural research, where, for instance, growing a plant from seed can be regarded as an experiment. But such applications, where statistical theory has achieved its greatest triumphs, are far away from economics; they come in,

---

[1] T. S. Ashton, *Economic and Social Investigations in Manchester* (1934) p. 3.

at the most, as part of the technological basis, external to economics, which, as we have seen, is implied in many, perhaps most, economic arguments.

The use of statistical methods in economics, as it was for about a century after 1833, was almost entirely descriptive; it was confined to the invention of measures, means of various kinds and measures of dispersion, by which large masses of figures could be summarized in manageable form. A little mathematics was required to elucidate the properties of such measures; but not much. The next step, the next relevant step, was the invention of sampling, which greatly increased the range of manageable material, in economics as well as in the sciences (where of course it also applies). Index-numbers, of prices or of production, are no more than samples; they do not actually average all the ratios of prices, or of quantities, that they purport to be averaging, only a sample of them. When we take them to represent the whole of what they purport to represent, we are relying, or should be relying, upon sampling theory—which is not at all a simple matter.

For already, when we seek to estimate characteristics of a 'parent' population from a sample, we are testing a hypothesis. The hypothesis that proportions in the parent population are the same as in the sample is just one hypothesis, to be tested against others. We are concerned with the probability that that hypothesis is correct. So sampling is a matter of the testing of hypotheses, the probability of hypotheses, 'inverse probability' as it has been called. It may indeed be maintained that all testing of hypotheses, that is to say, all inductions, partake of the nature of sampling. They are always a matter of proceeding from the observed cases to a larger 'population' of possible cases. So there is a sense in which the observed cases are a sample of possible cases.

I shall return to this question later; something must first be said on a question that is logically prior. What are we to mean, in this application and in others, by probability itself? There are two theories of probability—or it may be better to say there are two concepts of probability, for the mathematical structures that have been raised, on the basis of the one concept and on the other, seem largely to correspond. They are (1) the frequency theory and (2) the axiomatic theory, to give them their usual names. It is the frequency theory which has become orthodox; most modern works on statistical mathematics take it as their starting point. The chief proponents of the alternative approach have been Keynes, in his *Treatise on Probability* (1921) and Harold Jeffreys, in his *Theory of Probability* (1939). Jeffreys' version is more succinct, so I shall chiefly use it here. It is nevertheless significant that Keynes, the modern economist who has thought most deeply on these matters, was a proponent of the alternative theory. I have myself come to the view that the frequency theory, though it is thoroughly at home in many of the natural sciences, is not wide enough for economics. Indeed, on those points where Keynes and Jeffreys appear to differ, I generally find myself on the side of Keynes.[2]

According to the frequency theory, probability is a property of *random experiments*. 'Whenever we say that the probability of an event with respect to an experiment is equal to P' we mean that 'in a long series of repetitions of the experiment, it is practically

---

[2] In the preface to the third edition of his book (1960) Jeffreys claims that Keynes, in the paper on Ramsey that is included in *Essays in Biography*, had modified his views in Jeffreys' direction. I cannot see it. There is indeed a passage in Keynes's well-known QJE article of 1937 (Collected Writings XIV pp. 113–14) which strongly suggests the contrary.

certain that the frequency of E will be approximately equal to P.'[3] That is to say, the number of cases in which the outcome E occurs will approximate to a fraction P of the total number of experiments.

It is at once apparent that in order to make sense of the definition just quoted, we need to know what is meant by a 'repetition of the experiment'. If the repetitions were exact, the outcome of the second trial must be the same as that of the first, and so on. This, it is clear, is not what is being talked about. So the repetitions must not be exact; they must in some way be different, yet they must be repetitions. The differences between them must be *random*.

What is meant by random? No one, to my knowledge, has given a definition of random which does not refer back to some form of the above definition of probability.[4] So it is not easy to escape the reproach of circularity; if randomness and probability can only be defined, each in terms of the other, each is left undefined. There is no way out except to say that we do recognize, empirically, series of trials that do not repeat exactly, but which do appear to have the property that is expressed in the definition quoted. That such series exist, and are of the greatest importance, is beyond question; but if the basis of the theory is just this empirical recognition, we have no right to assume, without careful examination, that any series we choose to take will fit into that mould.

There clearly are cases, important in economics, in

---

[3] H. Cramér, *Mathematical Methods of Statistics*, p. 148. Cramér's statement is carefully devised to avoid pitfalls, so I think I am justified in following him.

[4] One cannot use the Bernouilli theorem to give a definition of random unless one already knows what one means by probability. Says the careful Cramér: 'It does not seem possible to give a precise definition of the word *random*.' (ibid. p. 138)

which we speak of probability in another sense. Cramér, whose frequency definition I have been quoting, was (apparently) writing the chapter of his book in which it occurs at the end of 1944; he himself gives, as an example of a 'probability' that would not fit into his definition, the probability that the European war would come to an end within a year.[5] This was a probability which, at that date, most people would have assessed to be a high one. But it is quite clear that it does not fall within the frequency definition; it is not a matter of trials that could be *repeated*.

We cannot avoid this other kind of probability in economics. Investments are made, securities are bought and sold, on a judgement of probabilities. This is true of economic behaviour; it is also true of economic theory. The probabilities of 'states of the world' that are formally used by economists, as for instance in portfolio theory, cannot be interpreted in terms of random experiments. Probability, in economics, must mean something wider.[6]

It need not, indeed should not, be so wide as to be irrational. Economic decisions are based on imperfect evidence, but they are based on some evidence. And they have a definite relation to the evidence they are based on. The economist, accordingly, is well-disposed towards Jeffreys' definition, which is first introduced as 'a valid primitive idea expressing the

---

[5] Ibid., p. 151.

[6] There is an interesting correspondence between the two concepts of probability, here contrasted, and the distinction between *Risk and Uncertainty*, made familiar to economists by F. H. Knight, in the title of whose book (1921) these words occur. Risks, according to Knight, arise from random sequences; so they can be covered, if there are enough of them, by insurance. True uncertainties, which he recognizes to be of greater importance in economics, cannot.

degree of confidence that we may reasonably have in a proposition, even though we may not be able to give either a deductive proof or a disproof of it. . . . It depends both on the proposition considered and on the data in relation to which it is considered'.[7] It looks very much as if this is what we want.

But it is quite a long road from this 'primitive idea' to statistical theory; it is as stages on that road that the 'axioms' are required. The first, put in less algebraic language than is employed by Jeffreys, states that, on given information, either one event[8] is more probable than another, or both are equally probable. The second is an axiom of transitivity. If, in the preceding sense, A is more probable than B, and B than C, then A is more probable than C.

The economist will notice the correspondence between the concept of probability, as it emerges from these two axioms, and his concept of utility. Modern utility theory begins with precisely similar postulates. As is well known, they provide nothing more than an ordinal relation. On the frequency definition, probability is unquestionably cardinal; but here it appears to be ordinal. Jeffreys, however, wishes to make it cardinal; this is the work of a further axiom (his axiom 4).[9]

The substance of axiom 4 can be put as follows. If (1) on the given information, A and B are exclusive

---

[7] Jeffreys, op. cit., p. 15.

[8] Jeffreys would say 'proposition', in order to cover the case, in which he is mainly interested, where the alternatives are hypotheses. I prefer, for reasons which will appear, to take that separately; so I shall boldly say 'events'.

[9] Axiom 3, like several of those which follow, is concerned with the relation between probability and certainty. This is not a matter of importance for my present discussion, so I shall leave it on one side.

alternatives, so that if A happens, B cannot happen (and *vice versa*), and if C and D are exclusive alternatives; and if (2), on the given information A and C are equally probable, while B and D are equally probable; then the occurrence of *either A or B*, and the occurrence of *either C or D*, must be equally probable. If this is granted, cardinality follows.

For if we represent the probability of A by an index a (which may initially be thought of as an ordinal index, like the utility index in Paretian ordinal theory), we must, since A and C are equally probable, represent the probability of C by the same index. And if we represent the probability of B by an index β, we must also represent the probability of D by β. Then, by axiom 4, if we represent the probability of *either A or B* by γ, we must also represent the probability of *either C or D* by γ. If this is granted, we shall *never go wrong* if we make $\gamma = a + \beta$. So axiom 4 is an additivity axiom. If we impose an additivity rule upon our indices, axiom 4 will always come out right.[10]

Once that is established, it is no more than a short step to say that if there are a number (say m) of equally probable and exclusive alternatives, each of which has probability a, the probability of one or other of them occurring is ma. So if we can divide these alternatives into groups, one containing m such units and the other n, the *relative probability* of one of the first group occurring to one of the second group occurring is m/n, which is unquestionably cardinal.

This is in fact what Jeffreys says;[11] but has he not gone back, at this point, to the classical theory of games of chance, in which the occurrence of a head

---

[10] It will be noticed that what corresponds to axiom 4 in utility theory is the particular assumption of independent utilities, which, as is well known, leads to cardinality.

[11] Jeffreys, op. cit., p. 23.

and that of a tail are taken to be 'equally probable'? It was just in order to avoid that nebulous concept that the frequency theory was invented. Has Jeffreys succeeded in making it less nebulous?

The trouble, in my view, is not with his axiom 4 but already with his axiom 1, the axiom which states that of two alternatives that are open on given information, either one is more probable than the other or both are equally probable. If two alternatives are equally probable, their *relative probability* is unity; this, in Jeffreys' construction, is clearly implied. But suppose that the information gives us no ground at all for ranking the alternatives; it is strictly irrelevant. This seems to me to be quite different from the case in which the information is relevant, but is *balanced*. That is to say, it tells us that A is in some way intermediate between alternatives which (if they were open) would be more probable than B, and others which would be less probable than B. It is the latter which is the more natural interpretation of *equally probable*. In the former, there is, on the evidence, no probability.[12]

Once this distinction is granted, a good many things fall into place. One can welcome Jeffreys' insistence that probability, in the widest sense, is a matter of judgement. If we call it subjective, that does not mean that it is, or can be, irrational; it is a matter of rational judgement, based on information, or on evidence. But the probabilities that may be so based are of various kinds, of which the particular kind which leads to cardinal probabilities, and so to a calculus of probabilities, is no more than one.

As an example of one that lies at other extreme,

---

[12] This is a matter which also has its counterpart in utility theory. See chapter 4 in 'The Logic of Order' in my *Revision of Demand Theory* (1956).

consider the following (which is an adaptation of Cramér's about the war coming to an end, which was noticed previously). Taking one's stance at the date when I am writing (October 1978), one would say that the probability of there *not* being a General Election in Britain before the end of 1979 was extremely small. Anyone with a knowledge of British institutions (the 'information' that is in question) would say that it is extremely small. But it is not zero, for the duration of a Parliament is governed by an Act of Parliament, which can be repealed by Parliament; there have indeed been three occasions, in 1716, in 1915 and in 1940, when a Parliament has prolonged its own life. Now set against this the probability that there will *not* be a Presidential Election in the United States before the end of 1980. Anyone with a knowledge of American institutions would say that this also is extremely improbable; but (with a knowledge of both British and American institutions both being reckoned as included in the 'information') he would surely add that in the American case the probability was even less. For it is much more difficult to change the electoral calendar in the United States than in Britain; in the whole of the history of the Union it has never been done. It was not done even in the midst of the Civil War, in 1864. So it is fair to say that these probabilities can be ordered. But there is no way of varying parameters (as by changing the dates of 1979 and 1980 which have been introduced into the statements) so as to make them respectively greater and less than some probabilities which we assess to be equal.[13]

---

[13] It is indeed true that since, in the British case, an election before the end of 1978 is (at the time of writing) highly improbable, and an election before the end of 1979 is highly probable, an election before the middle of 1979 should have a probability that is intermediate. So, by vary-

Cases like this do arise in economics (consider the probability that some regulation, at present in force, may be changed); but it is perhaps more usual for the assessments to relate to a continuum. This, from the point of view of Jeffreys' first axiom, looks more promising; but how much does it help?

Consider the case of price-expectations: the expectation, for instance, of what the pound-dollar exchange rate will be at the end of next week. It is tempting (and how often do economists fall into the temptation) to say that there will, on given information, be a particular 'expected' rate r*, which is such that (1) for *any* rate r_1 which is greater than r*, the probability of an outcome above r_1 is less than the probability of an outcome below it, and (2) that for *any* rate r_2 which is less than r*, the probability of an outcome less than r_2 is less than the probability of an outcome above it. One can say that, it will be noted, without assuming that one can set numerical values upon these probabilities; one needs that further step, and the assumption that these numerical probabilities are normally distributed, before one can describe the state of expectation in terms of mean and variance, in the standard statistical manner.[14]

---

ing the date, we should be able to generate a scale of probabilities. But this does not help. For I am saying that the probability of an election in Britain before the end of 1979 is high, but is less than that of the American with which I have compared it. One cannot make these probabilities equal by extending the British date into 1980 or beyond. The British probability would always be less than the American, whatever date was mentioned in the statement.

[14] In my own work on portfolio theory, I began with a version that ran in terms of means and variances (Essay 6 in my *Critical Essay in Monetary Theory*, 1967). But I came to feel that there was something wrong with it; and that the

But let us go back to the first step: can it be accepted? Why should the statements which I have just been numbering be acceptable for *any* r_1 and r_2? Why should it not be the case[15] that there are two values, outside of which probabilities are clear, while there is a grey zone, within which they are unclear, in between? That is to say, for any r_1 which is $> r_1{}^*$, the probability of a still higher value is less than the probability of one that is below it; while for any r_2 which is $< r_2{}^*$, the probability of a value less than that r_2 is similarly outweighed. All this, as before, save that $r_1{}^*$, and $r_2{}^*$ are not equal but $r_1{}^* > r_2{}^*$. Anywhere in the grey zone, there is no probability either way; the evidence is insufficient to establish a probability.

Common sense would suggest that this latter may well be a better description of a prospect that is based upon imperfect evidence;[16] though it may well be that one should go further, attributing some form of uncertainty to the end-points $r_1{}^*$ and $r_2{}^*$ themselves.[17] But it is sufficient for my purpose to treat them as firm. For as soon as we admit a grey zone, whatever we say about its end-points, it is straightaway impossible that both of Jeffreys' axioms—his axiom 1 and his axiom 4—can hold. Take any two different values that fall within the grey zone; call them g_1 and g_2, with $g_1 > g_2$.

---

same applied to the versions, in similar terms, that have been put forward by others. My second attempt ('The Disaster Point in Risk Theory', *Economic Perspectives*, 1977) though still formally written in terms of numerical probabilities, is much less dependent on them. The probability of disaster, on which that later version turns, does not have to be numerical.

[15] See Figure 3 overleaf.

[16] We have already found an example in our discussion of Keynesian liquidity in chapter VII above.

[17] William Fellner, in his *Probability and Profit* (1965) did a good deal of thinking in that direction.

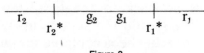

Figure 3

Then values above g_1 are not more probable than values below it; and values below g_1 are not more probable than values above it. So, on axiom 1, we ought to say that they are equally probable. And the same will hold for g_2. But values below g_1 include those below g_2 and those between g_1 and g_2; so, on axiom 4, if above g_1 and below g_1 are equally probable, above g_2 and below g_2 cannot be equally probable. We have transcended Jeffreys' axioms, because we have included a case in which inadequacy of evidence makes probabilities non-comparable. There seems to be no reason in general, and particularly in economics, why cases such as this should not be contemplated.

One may then sum up in the following way. We may take as the general definition of probability Jeffreys' 'primitive notion'—the degree of confidence that may reasonably be expressed in a proposition on the basis of given evidence. But we must then re-write his first axiom. We must say that of two alternatives, on given evidence, either A is more probable than B, or B more probable than A, or they are equally probable, *or that they are not comparable*. That makes probabilities partially, but not completely, orderable. (Thinking of the analogy with the indifference curves of utility theory, an indifference curve may be *thick*.) There is, however, a sub-class of such assessments, in which information is sufficient for a judgement of greater, or less, or equal, to be always possible. And there is a sub-class of these in which exclusive alternatives can be distinguished, so that it is possible for axiom 4 to hold. We may then, but only then, accept the whole of Jeffreys' reasoning, and grant that the probabilities that emerge in that case can be numerically expressed. The way is then open to the probability calculus; but it is only in this sub-class, out of the wider class of cases to which the general notion of probability can be applied, that we can proceed to the calculus. We may grant that in the natural sciences (particularly because of the 'static' character which we formerly saw cause to attribute to them[18]) this sub-class is of enormous importance. But it remains a sub-class; it is not all-inclusive.[19]

---

[18] See above, pp. x–xi.

[19] What I am saying may more readily be apprehended if it is illustrated pictorially.

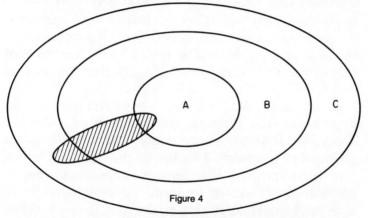

Figure 4

A is the field where probabilities are unquestionably numerical—the classical field of games of chance, and of random experiments (or observations of what is accepted to be the same phenomenon). The ring B is that in which probabilities are orderable, but not expressible as numbers. The ring C is that in which they are not even orderable, or not completely orderable.

I am maintaining (1) that even in ring C probability judgements can sometimes be made, and that they can be rational since it is conceivable that they could be improved by additional evidence (2) that the field of economics has the character of the shaded area, some part of it being in A, some in B, and some in C.

It is not at all surprising that the sub-class, thus identified, turns out to be co-terminous with that to which, as we have seen, the frequency theory applies. For on either approach, all that is asserted, or should be asserted, is that we do, very often, have to deal with what are in effect random series, or are reducible to random series. But it is not inevitable that our data should be of that character; even when they are not, probability still has a meaning.

Whether a particular series, such as one of the time-series which concern us so much in economics, is properly to be regarded as a random series, is itself a question that requires to be examined. It is itself a hypothesis that needs to be tested. But can such a question, which concerns the applicability of the probability calculus, be tested by the methods of that calculus? It is not at all obvious that that can be done.

Much has been written about judgement on hypotheses, the fundamental problem of inductive logic. For Jeffreys, as for many others, it is itself a probability problem. The Bayes theorem, on which (on that approach) that logic is supposed to rest, is conventionally stated in terms of numerical probabilities. I shall take the statement of it, in those terms, for granted; since the important question, from my point of view, is the extent to which the argument can be extended to cover probabilities which are not numerical, but can be ordered, or (as we have seen) partially ordered. The question itself is then no more than an ordinal question, of the grounds on which we may prefer one hypothesis to another.

Even so, we get a hint from the Bayesian analysis, which teaches us to distinguish between the Prior Probability—the probability of the hypothesis on general information—and what is now called the Likelihood, which is the probability of the occurrence of the particular events (on which the hypothesis is being tested) as it would be if the hypothesis in question were correct. That distinction is always useful; it is not only in the case (beloved of scientists and, as we shall see, of econometrists) when prior probabilities are equal, so that we can make a decision on Maximum Likelihood, without reference to prior probability, that the distinction holds. There is no reason, in general, why prior probabilities should not be distinguishable. If prior probability goes one way, and likelihood the other, we have no rule for making a decision. Our judgement nonetheless may be clarified.

Looking for an example as far away from numerical probabilities as possible I may take the case of textual criticism. The hypotheses that are being compared are alternative readings. We suspect that the received reading, that which has come down to us from ancient manuscripts or from the earliest printed versions, is not what the poet wrote, or what he intended. An emendation is accordingly suggested, which, it is claimed, makes better sense, or is more in his style. That is a claim that the emendation has greater prior probability. There are two hypotheses (1) that the received text is correct (2) that the emended text is correct; they are being compared, so far, as if they were on a par. It used to be thought that that was enough; but it is now admitted that if the emendation is to be accepted, or is just to be persuasive, it must face a further test. We have the fact that it is the received text that has come down to us; if the received text is correct, this needs no further explanation; but if the emended text is correct, there is a transmission problem, which is a question of Likelihood. It must always be the received text which has the greater Likelihood, just because it requires no further explanation. But if it can be shown that corruption from the emended text supposed correct is not much less probable than an uncorrupted transmission, a strong prior probability for the emendation may carry the day. This is indeed a matter of judgement, the weighing up of one difference in probabilities against another; there is no rule by which we can shelve responsibility for it. But it is judgement that can be improved by further information; thus the case for the emendation will be improved if it can be shown that mistakes, of the kind which it has had to suppose to have occurred in the transmission, are on other evidence quite common.

It may well happen, even in the natural sciences, that prior probabilities are not equal, so that similar issues come up. Take the case, already considered in a previous chapter,[20] when a 'fact' (some new information) is supposed to confute a theory, a previously established theory. By saying that the theory was well established, we imply that the probability of its truth, on previous information, was high; its prior probability was high. But when it is tested against the new information, its Likelihood is low, perhaps very low indeed. A so-called 'ad hoc' theory, which is directly devised to meet the new information, will have a much higher Likelihood; but (on the old information) its Prior Probability is small. We have then no rule for deciding between them. Not until a theory has been invented which can cope with the whole of the evidence, so that its Prior Probability is not less than that of the old theory, while its Likelihood is greater, does it become clear that the new theory has to take over. That was what was said, in other terms, when we came to the issue before;[21] it fits in.

There is however another way (a more revealing

---

[20] See above, p. 33.
[21] See above, p. 34.

way) in which an 'ad hoc' theory may fail to be acceptable. Suppose that it is not inconsistent with the old information; it is simply that it is irrelevant to the old information. Now we do not say that in this case Prior Probabilities are equal, so that we can take a decision on the rule of Maximum Likelihood, taken by itself. That would always make the decision go in favour of the 'ad hoc' theory, even though it meant throwing all that we knew before, or thought that we knew before, out of the window. Since there is no means of judging the prior probabilities, we suspend judgement. And it would surely be accepted that we are right to do so.

It follows, accordingly, that it is not sufficient, in order that a correct decision should be attainable on the principle of Maximum Likelihood, taken as sole test, that there should be no prior probability, one way or the other; it is necessary that we should have some ground for supposing that prior probabilities are equal. I am not in the least denying that there are many cases, very many cases, very many important cases, when the view that they are equal is quite acceptable; it is just that to say we have no knowledge about prior probabilities is not enough. It is just the same as with the probabilities of events, which I was formerly discussing.[22]

The most obvious cases in which it is fair to proceed, from ignorance to equality of prior probabilities, and thence to the rule of Maximum Likelihood, are precisely those that partake of the nature of experiment, in which experience has shown that there is a random element. Precisely those to which the frequency view applies! So it is not at all surprising that scientists, who work with such experiments, have a natural leaning towards the frequency theory. In their world it applies; but does it in economics?

---

[22] See above, p. 110.

It may readily be granted that there are some parts of economics to which it does apply. When we are looking for a conclusion that is to be derived from sampling (as for instance in the study of family budgets) it is possible to take steps to ensure that the sample is random, or at least fairly random; we then have a right to make use of sampling theory, which (as explained) is a branch of the probability calculus. The means and variances that are calculated from the sample do then have a meaning, which is relevant to the questions that are being asked.

Things become more difficult when we turn to time-series, which is the application which in economics we most often want to make. Even here there are some time-series that may plausibly be treated as independent observations. This holds, or may hold (as previously explained)[28] in some simple cases of demand study, where the carry-over from one period to another is not important. The econometrist, who works in that field, may claim that he is not treading on very shaky ground. But if one asks him what he is really doing, he will not find it easy, even here, to give a convincing answer. If, as is likely, he thinks himself to be working with a frequency concept of probability, he must be treating the observations known to him (extending, say, from 1960 to 1977) as a sample of a larger 'population'; but what population? The observations which may be made, if the inquiry continues, at future dates? He will want a long series, extending, perhaps, to the year 2100. But how much bearing have means and variances that are calculated for this long series on what will really happen—not just on what, in the mathematical sense, is 'expected' to happen—in 1979 and 1980, the years immediately ahead?

---

[23] See above, p. 66.

If, as in terms of what has been said in this chapter would seem to be wiser, he bases himself on a confidence notion of probability, he is somewhat safer. But it is then not clear that he has any right to make predictions in the form of an 'expectation', subject to confidence limits'±'. The confidence limits, on this interpretation, have much more meaning than the 'expected' value, conventionally half-way between them. It makes sense to say that an outcome, outside the confidence limits, is improbable. But there is no reason to attach much importance to the central value, unless we are prepared to accept Jeffreys' axioms, which (as was shown) do not, in such cases as this, have much appeal. There is no reason why the central value should not fall within a 'grey zone'. But it is hard not to give it more importance than it deserves.

When we cannot accept that the observations, along the time-series available to us, are independent, or cannot by some device be divided into groups that can be treated as independent, we get into much deeper water. For we have then, in strict logic, no more than one observation, all of the separate items having to be taken together. For the analysis of that the probability calculus is useless; it does not apply. We are left to use our judgement, making sense of what has happened as best we can, in the manner of the historian. Applied economics does then come back to history, after all.

I am bold enough to conclude, from these considerations that the usefulness of 'statistical' or 'stochastic' methods in economics is a good deal less than is now conventionally supposed. We have no business to turn to them automatically; we should always ask ourselves, before we apply them, whether they are appropriate to the problem in hand. Very often they are not. Thus it is not at all sensible to take a small number of observations (sometimes no more than a dozen observations) and to use the rules of probability theory to deduce from them a 'significant' general law. For we are assuming, if we do so, that the variations from one to another of the observations are random, so that if we had a larger sample (as we do not) they would by some averaging tend to disappear. But what nonsense this is when the observations are derived, as not infrequently happens, from different countries, or localities, or industries—entities about which we may well have relevant information, but which we have deliberately decided, by our procedure, to ignore. By all means let us plot the points on a chart, and try to explain them; but it does not help in explaining them to suppress their names. The probability calculus is no excuse for forgetfulness.

Index

DATE DUE

AUG 2 5 1983			